HEALING YOUR HORSE

HEALING YOUR HORSE

ALTERNATIVE THERAPIES

MEREDITH L. SNADER, V.M.D.

SHARON L. WILLOUGHBY, D.V.M., D.C.

DEVA KAUR KHALSA, V.M.D.

CRAIG DENEGA

IHOR JOHN BASKO, D.V.M.

HOWELL
BOOK HOUSE

NEW YORK

Macmillan General Reference
A Simon & Schuster Macmillan Company
1633 Broadway
New York, NY 10019-6785

Library of Congress Cataloging-in-Publication Data
Healing your horse : alternative therapies / Meredith L. Snader.
p.   cm.
Includes index.
ISBN 0-87605-829-2
1. Horses—Diseases—Alternative treatment.   I. Snader, Meredith L.
SF951.H44   1993
636.1′08953—dc20   93-2682   CIP

10   9   8   7

Printed in the United States of America

It matters not whether medicine is old or new,
    so long as it brings about a cure.
It matters not whether theories be Eastern or Western,
    so long as they prove to be true.
                                            Jen Hsou Lin

CONTENTS

INTRODUCTION

Performance horses, like human athletes, are pressured to achieve their maximum potential. They are trained, fed, and cared for so they can go faster, jump higher, and run longer. The daily routines of training result in frequent injuries and aches and pains that, if not controlled or eliminated, impede performance and disappoint expectations. Many owners and trainers have resorted to the use of drugs that allow horses to compete despite their physical discomfort. Unfortunately, some of the drugs do not remedy the problem but merely mask its symptoms, allowing the horse to continue racing or jumping, for example, while possibly incurring permanent injury. To counter the misuse of drugs, stringent regulations have been enacted for the treatment of race horses and show horses to prevent abuse of these equine athletes.

Increasingly, owners and trainers, dissatisfied with drugs and the "quick fixes" offered by conventional medicine, are turning to alternative therapies, specifically, to acupuncture, massage, herbology, chiropractic, and homeopathy. Each of these therapies, alone or in combination, provides natural cures without the risk of abuse.

Acupuncture, massage, herbology, chiropractic, and homeopathy evolved from ancient Asian healing traditions introduced more than 3,000 years ago to help the body use its inherent recuperative powers to achieve healing. These sciences have proved themselves effective over the centuries.

Numerous old treatment regimens described in early veterinary texts utilize the principles of acupuncture, massage, herbology, chiropractic, and homeopathy. The majority of the present-day medical community, however, is of the opinion that we have progressed far beyond these ancient and dated practices to a world of modern approaches such as nuclear medicine, laser surgery, and a broad spectrum of antibiotics to be used for equine care. A minority is of the opinion that ancient practitioners were able to achieve equal success in many conditions by using natural compounds, by balancing the body's energy, and by manipulating the body. The old saying, "The past holds the key to the future," is valid for medicine as well. Fortunately, some equine practitioners today recognize that many ailments that do not respond to the most advanced techniques of traditional medicine are responsive to the ancient healing arts.

To be sure, these ancient arts alone are not the solution for every condition or for every horse. Consequently, we advise you to ask your veterinarian to perform a complete examination for an additional diagnosis beyond what might be offered in this book. Many conditions that appear simple may be manifestations of deeper problems requiring one of the more modern modalities. By failing to seek professional help, you may allow severe problems to arise. Once a diagnosis is confirmed, however, the alternative therapies described here may be applied as an adjunct to conventional treatment. Together they may help your horse recover faster and restore him to health and his full athletic potential.

Each of the sections in this book is written by a practitioner who specializes in that particular therapy for treating equine athletes. Each of the authors presents an overview of his or her therapy and demonstrates how each technique works to promote self-healing, good health, and increased performance. Perhaps among them you will find that key from the past that will unlock the door to your horse's future.

MEREDITH L. SNADER, V.M.D.

HEALING
YOUR
HORSE

ACUPUNCTURE

MEREDITH L. SNADER, V.M.D.

INTRODUCTION

For over 3,000 years the Chinese have used acupuncture in the treatment of horses, an impressive historic testimony to its usefulness and effectiveness. However, it was not until the 1970s, with the political opening of China, that people in the United States showed any real interest in acupuncture. This interest prompted scientific inquiries by Western veterinarians into the applications of acupuncture for the treatment of horses. Investigation showed that acupuncture constitutes a safe treatment for many equine conditions that were previously difficult to treat with conventional therapy. Consequently, over the last twenty years an increasing number of veterinarians have become aware of the usefulness of acupuncture and have incorporated it into their practice. In 1989 the American Veterinary Medical Association recognized acupuncture as a "valid modality and an integral part of veterinary medicine."[1] This technique, however, is considered a medical procedure to be practiced only by licensed veterinarians.

The public in general has begun to appreciate a more holistic approach to veterinary medicine. This development, coupled with the advent of more stringent rules governing medication in the horse industry, has led many owners and trainers to seek alternative therapies. Acupuncture may be the ancient answer to a modern dilemma.

• HISTORY •

Veterinary acupuncture is as old as acupuncture itself. A three-thousand-year-old chart of an elephant, found in Sri Lanka, offers the earliest documented evidence of its use. We know that Chinese veterinary acupuncture was first practiced in the Shang Dynasty (c. 1600 B.C.–c. 1050 B.C.). Chao Fu (947 B.C.–928 B.C.), an expert on animal diseases in the Chou Dynasty (c. 1066 B.C.–221 B.C.), is the earliest recorded doctor of veterinary medicine.[2]

Shun Yang (Pao Lo), who lived about 480 B.C., was the first recorded full-time practitioner of Chinese veterinary medicine and as such is considered the Father of veterinary acupuncture.[3]

During the Spring and Autumn Warring period (403 B.C.–221 B.C.), the *Huang Ti Nei Ching* (Yellow Emperor's Classic on Internal Medicine), one of the oldest known documents and the bible of traditional Chinese medicine, was compiled. It discusses the Oriental philosophies of anatomy, physiology, pathology, diagnosis, and treatment of maladies. It describes, for example, how the flow of blood throughout the body is controlled by the heart—the same discovery William Harvey made for Western medicine in 1628. The *Nei Ching* also discusses the establishment of meridians, the location of 361 body points, prescriptions for various diseases, needle shapes and sizes, and distribution of forbidden points. This book, which has been translated into English, is esteemed for its longevity as well as for its scientific interest. It has survived political upheavals and revolutions and is a timeless work on which each generation has left its mark.[3]

In the Ch'in and Han dynasties (221 B.C.–A.D. 220) the practice of veterinary medicine has been verified by the finding of prescriptions written on wood strips which describe acupuncture and the kind and quantities of herbs to be used in herbal treatments. A rock carving from this era shows soldiers acupuncturing their horses with arrows to stimulate them before battle.[2]

A great many horses were raised for military requirements during the T'ang Dynasty (A.D. 618–907), and most of the books written during this period deal with diseases of horses. One of these treatises, the *Golden Prescriptions*, introduced the *tsun (cun)*, a unit of measurement used in acupuncture for both humans and animals. The T'ang rulers formalized veterinary medical education by establishing the first veterinary school.[3]

Traditional Chinese medicine divided the medical professionals into four categories: physicians, surgeons, veterinarians, and dieticians. Training and practices in these disciplines overlapped to some degree, and so different kinds of services could be performed by the same person. Government personnel and "barefoot veterinarians" (paraveterinary medical personnel) have treated cows, horses, pigs, and chickens for more than two thousand years. Animals were essential for military maneuvers and sustenance. Dogs and cats were not important in Chinese culture and consequently no evidence of charts or prescriptions for these animals exist before the seventeenth century.[2]

Jesuits who had served in the Chinese courts introduced acupuncture into France in the seventeenth century and it was used there until the nineteenth century. Revived in the twentieth century, acupuncture spread to Austria and Germany. In 1956 Oswald Kothbauer, an Austrian veterinarian, began experimenting with acupuncture in cattle by injecting irritating substances into various organs to identify corresponding active points.[3]

Acupuncture was introduced into the United States about a century ago with the importation of Chinese laborers, but its practice was limited to the Chinese community. This changed in the 1970s, when China's opening to the West created an intense interest in all facets of Chinese life and culture. One result has been an awareness of the opportunities that acupuncture has to offer in both diagnosis and therapy.

In 1974, as a direct result of increasing global interest, Dr. Grady Young, a veterinarian from Thomasville, Georgia, founded the International Veterinary Acupuncture Society "to promote excellence in the practice of Veterinary Acupuncture as an integral part of a total veterinary health care delivery system."[5]

· WHAT IS ACUPUNCTURE? ·

Acupuncture is the insertion of fine needles into specific predetermined points on the surface of the body in order to regulate bodily functions.

According to traditional Chinese medicine there is a flow of energy called Chi, consisting of positive (Yang) and negative (Yin) components that course through channels in the body called meridians. Imbalances of energy levels between the positive (Yang) and the negative (Yin) and blockages in the meridians allow pathological conditions to begin. External factors (wind, cold, heat), emotional factors (fear, anger, stress), and pathogenic factors (trauma, exertion, impaired circulation) play an important role in creating these imbalances. By stimulating specific acupuncture points or a combination of such points, one is able to adjust the energy level, reestablish a homeostatic condition (equilibrium), and allow healing to take place.[2]

▪ WHAT ARE ACUPUNCTURE POINTS? ▪

An acupuncture point is an area of the skin 1 to 2 mm in size located over specific anatomic landmarks in small indentations or nodules on the body that are linked with visceral organs. The acupuncture point has a greater density of neuroreceptors than in adjacent tissue.

There are three types of acupuncture points. The primary ones are found along the routes of large nerves in the skin and muscle. The secondary points are found in smaller nerves, and the third type are found at small nerve-muscle fibers. When half the primary points are painful the horse may appear uncomfortable. Progression of pain to secondary points makes the animal very uncomfortable and reactivity on all three types makes him difficult to handle. Pathological changes occurring in affected organs increases blood flow, which results in lowered electrical resistance, and increased sensitivity at the acupuncture points. These tender "trigger" points may be produced by muscle spasms, tension, or endocrine imbalance.[4]

There is evidence that acupuncture points have a role in healing, not only locally but at distant areas. They have a regulatory effect on the internal organs and can both increase and decrease organs' functioning. Therefore, the selection of points and the type of stimulation applied are critical to the success of the acupuncture.[6]

There appear to be 361 traditional acupuncture points located on twelve paired and two unpaired meridians in the human body. In addition, there are extra points that do not lie over traditional meridians, but are effective in treating certain diseases and points located in the ear. All points are divided into two categories based on therapeutic properties: *local* points, which treat diseases in a neighboring or local area, and *distant* points, which treat conditions in remote areas. Points are further categorized as *permanent* and *temporary*. Permanent points exist all the time and are on meridians or extra points. Temporary points are not on meridians and appear only when a pathological process occurs, such as Ashi points or tender spots.

In horses there are approximately thirteen categories of specific points, which have special properties and are grouped under special names. By combining these points, an acupuncturist is able to formulate a prescription for any disease or lameness that may be present.

1. *Mu or Alarm Points*   Located on the abdomen and chest, in the vicinity of a particular organ. They often become tender when the associated organ is diseased.

2. *Terminal Points*   Found at the beginning and end of each meridian.

3. *Tonification Points and Sedation Points*   Increase and decrease energy in the meridian.

4. *Source Points*   Located in the knees and hocks. These points increase the effect of the tonification and sedation points.

5. *Connecting Points*   Connect the coupled meridians and equalize the Chi between them.

6. *Shu or Association Points*   Located parallel to the spine. They run along the back, starting behind the scapula and ending in the middle of the sacrum. These points are located on the Bladder meridian, and each point is named for a meridian. The points become tender when a pathological condition

arises either in a specific organ or along the meridian. In the horse these points are the most important of all the special points, as they are frequently used in diagnosing and treating lameness and disease.

7. *Command Points*   Found below the elbow and stifle.

8. *Special Action Points*   Points that have a special effect on certain specific conditions.

9. *Horary Points*   Points used during the time when energy flow is greatest in the meridian.

10. *Trigger Points*   Specific points that appear during the course of disease or trauma. These points disappear as the condition subsides.

11. *Auricular Points*   Special points located in the ear that represent all areas of the body.

12. *Accumulation Points*   Located on each of the twelve meridians where the energy level is the greatest.

13. *Master Points*   Represent the four major areas of the body: (1) the face, (2) the chest, (3) the abdomen and digestive system, and (4) the back and lumbar area.

On human charts many of these specific points fall between the wrist and fingers, ankles and toes. Owing to anatomical differences between the human being and the horse, there are fewer acupuncture points in the horse, which over the course of time has evolved only one digit arising from the carpal and tarsal joint. This fact has caused much discrepancy in the mapping of traditional end points. Treatment of many of these points in the horse is not tolerated well.

Points can be located by feeling with your fingers for small indentations or by using a "point finder." This instrument locates acupuncture points by indicating areas of lower electrical resistance and higher conductance on the skin. Using this instrument on animals often produces unreliable results because of the interference of hair and skin moisture.

• WHAT IS CHI? •

In traditional Chinese medicine, Chi denotes both the essential substances of the body that maintain its vital activity, and the functional activities of the principal organs and tissues. Chi is too rarefied to be seen; it manifests itself only in the functioning of the organs. All vital activities of the body are explained by movement of Chi. Chi is divided into four types: Congenital Chi, Pectoral Chi, Defensive Chi, and Nutritive Chi. Congenital Chi is inherited from the parents and is located primarily in the kidneys. The other three types—known collectively as Acquired Chi— are derived after birth from food. Congenital Chi and the three Acquired Chi depend upon each other for their production and nourishment.[7]

• THEORY OF YIN AND YANG •

The ancient Chinese people, in the course of their everyday life and work, explained all aspects of the natural world as having dual and opposing aspects, such as day and night, movement and stillness, and hot and cold. Yang and Yin are the terms that express these dual and opposite qualities. Yang is the male principle, denoting light and activity; Yin is the female principle, denoting darkness and passivity. All the meridians are assigned a role as either Yang or Yin.[7]

ZANG AND FU ORGANS

Zang (Yin) and Fu (Yang) are the general terms for the organs of the body. The six Zang organs are the Lungs, Spleen, Heart, Kidneys, Pericardium, and Liver. The main function of these organs is to manufacture and store essential substances, including Chi (the vital essence), blood, and body fluids. The six Fu organs are the Large Intestine, Stomach, Small Intestine, Bladder, Tripleheater, and Gall Bladder. Their main function is to receive and digest food and to transmit and excrete waste. The Zang-Fu organs are located inside the body, but their physiological action and pathological changes are observable externally.[7]

THE FIVE ELEMENTS

The five-element theory is another explanation of the nature of the Zang-Fu organs and the relationships among them. The five elements refer to the five categories in the natural world: Wood, Fire, Earth, Metal, and Water. According to the theory, all phenomena in nature correspond to one of these elements, which are in a constant state of motion and change. These five elements are dependent upon each other and are inseparable. Each coupled meridian (Yin-Yang) is associated with an element, except for the Fire element which has two coupled meridians. These elements are plotted in a cyclical chart called the creation cycle, which depicts the flow of energy from meridian to meridian or from element to element.[7]

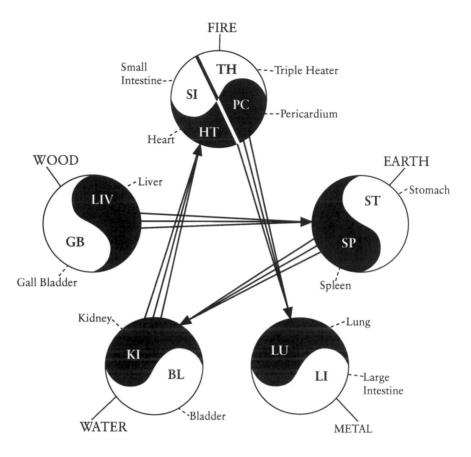

WHAT ARE MERIDIANS?

In Chinese traditional medicine, meridians are pathways in the body in which Chi and blood circulate. As mentioned earlier, there are twelve paired and two unpaired meridians. The paired meridians are distributed symmetrically over the entire body. The meridians connect internally with the Zang-Fu organs and externally with the joints, limbs, sense organs, and other superficial tissues of the body. Not surprisingly, the meridians are divided into six Yin and six Yang meridians. The Yin meridians are the Lungs, Spleen, Heart, Kidneys, Pericardium, and Liver.

The Yang meridians are the Large Intestine, Stomach, Small Intestine, Bladder, Triple Heater, and Gall Bladder. Each Yin meridian is coupled with a Yang meridian in a female-male relationship. The Yin meridians course along the inside of an extremity while the Yang meridians run along the outside.[7]

In the horse, the three Yin meridians of the forelimb flow from the chest to the foot, where they meet the three Yang meridians and ascend to the head. The three Yang meridians of the hind limb start at the head and descend to the hind foot, where they meet the three Yin meridians and flow upward to the chest where they join the three Yin meridians of the forelimb. This completes the cycle of energy flow in the body.

Most acupuncture points are located along these meridians. Traditional Chinese acupuncture charts of animals are available for the horse, the pig, fowl, and cattle. Although the meridian system is mentioned briefly in some ancient Chinese texts, most points are described independent from one another, not lying on meridians, and are identified only by name and number.[8]

The human acupuncture system based on meridian concepts is much more organized and easier to learn than the traditional methods for animals based on random points. Once the human system is mastered, its principles can be applied to animals by transposing anatomical locations and functions. This system is the one in current use for horses. The evolutionary loss of toes in the horse has created difficulty in locating points below the knee (carpus) and hock (tarsus). It is best to use the traditional random points in these areas.[9]

▪ THE SCIENTIFIC BASIS ▪
OF ACUPUNCTURE

Many medical scientists in the early 1970s assumed that acupuncture worked as a placebo. But how does one explain the use of a mere placebo in veterinary acupuncture for more than 2,000 years? Animals are not suggestible and very few are capable of hypnosis. As a result, in the past twenty-five years scientists have been investigating two important questions: Does acupuncture really work, and if so, what are its mechanisms?

The ancient Chinese may have been very astute when they stated that external acupuncture points and meridians are connected with internal organs. The superficial pain felt in diseases of the organs occurs where sensory nerves and segmental nerves from the viscera enter the spinal cord. Cutaneous stimulation of acupuncture points is transmitted to the internal viscera through the spinal cord. At the nerve endings either the parasympathetic or the sympathetic components are stimulated selectively and the function of the autonomic nervous system is regulated. In classical terms, "stimulation" refers to activation of the sympathetic system, while "sedation" refers to parasympathetic activation.

One of the earliest attempts to explain acupuncture was the "gate theory." This theory, proposed by Melzack and Wall, states that when large nerve fibers carrying sensations of pressure and touch are stimulated, they block pain sensation carried by small nerve fibers. This hypothetical gate prevents pain from being transmitted higher in the central nervous system, therefore no perception of pain can take place. True, acupuncture points may represent an area where a greater number of large and small fibers converge, but the gate theory does not fully explain why the effects of acupuncture last so long or how acupuncture eliminates chronic pain.[2]

Current opinion about the efficacy of acupuncture com-

HOW ACUPUNCTURE WORKS

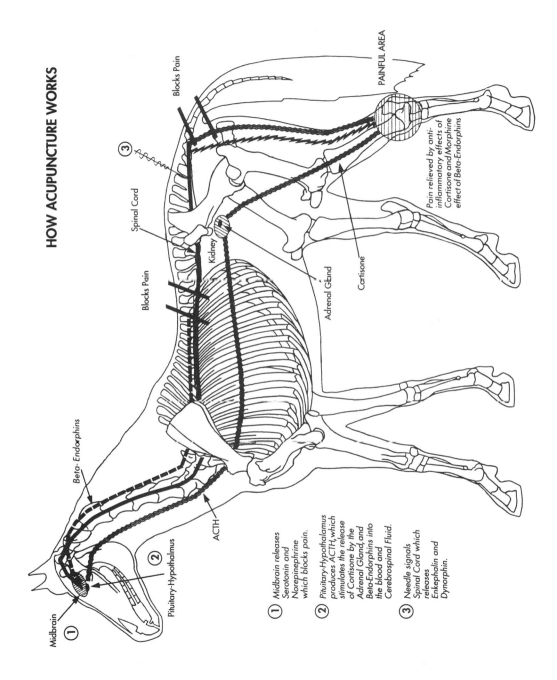

PAINFUL AREA

Blocks Pain

③

Spinal Cord

Blocks Pain

Kidney

Adrenal Gland

Cortisone

Pain relieved by anti-inflammatory effects of Cortisone and Morphine effect of Beta-Endorphins

Beta-Endorphins

Pituitary-Hypothalmus

ACTH

Midbrain

①

②

① Midbrain releases Serotonin and Norepinephrine which blocks pain.

② Pituitary-Hypothalamus produces ACTH, which stimulates the release of Cortisone by the Adrenal Gland, and Beta-Endorphins into the blood and Cerebrospinal Fluid.

③ Needle signals Spinal Cord which releases Enkephalin and Dynorphin.

bines humoral and neurologic theories; it holds that stimulation of acupuncture points—by use of a needle, pressure, heat, or electricity—activates nerve fibers in the muscle. Impulses then travel through small myelinated fibers (fibers sheathed in a fatty substance) to three centers: the spinal cord, midbrain and the pituitary hypothalamus.[10]

In the spinal cord there is a release of the endorphins enkephalin and dynorphin. These substances prevent the transmission of painful stimuli to the spinal cord. When painful stimuli ascend from the spinal cord to the midbrain, enkephalins are released that signal the release of two monoamines, serotonin and norepinephrine. These substances travel down a descending pathway to the spinal cord, where they act synergistically to block pain transmission from the spinal cord. Activation of the hypothalamus-pituitary releases beta-endorphins and ACTH (adrenocorticotropic hormone) into the blood and cerebrospinal fluid, causing analgesia at a distance. The ACTH travels to the adrenal cortex, where cortisol, a steroid produced by the body, is released into the blood. (Cortisol is similar in composition to such anti-inflammatory medications as Azium, which may explain why acupuncture is helpful in blocking the inflammation of arthritis.)[10]

What is the practical significance of this three-cornered theory involving the spinal cord, midbrain, and hypothalamus? Needles placed near the site of pain activate all three areas to release endorphins. When needles are placed far away from the painful region, they activate the midbrain and hypothalamus to provide pain relief throughout the body. Local needling usually gives a more intensive relief than distant needling because it activates all three centers. Local and distal needling act synergistically to augment pain relief.

In 1942 two Canadian psychiatrists discovered memory banks in pain-receiving cells. Chronic pain is said to be the storage of original pain after an injury has healed.

Acupuncture is said to produce a memory loss in these pain-receiving cells, thereby diminishing or obliterating chronic pain.[2] These pain-receiving cells may be activated by changes in barometric pressure, which is perhaps why chronic pain seems to be often weather-related.[10]

• TECHNIQUES •

There are many fascinating parallels between modern veterinary practice and the ancient Chinese methods of stimulation. Techniques vary greatly—from the earliest, such as needling and moxibustion (applying caustic herbs to the skin), to the more modern, such as laser treatment and implantation. Each method will be described.

NEEDLES

From ancient times until about four thousand years ago, stone instruments were used to achieve pain relief through bloodletting. Then, with the development of bronze casting three thousand years ago, bronze needles came to be used. According to the *Nei Ching*, the earliest acupuncture needles were composed of copper-wire handles and shafts worked from the metal of a horse's bit. Next, iron needles were used. The most widely used material today is stainless steel because of its strength, resistance to corrosion, and ease of sterilization.[11]

The acupuncture needle is composed of a handle and a pointed shaft. The handle permits greater ease in manipulating the shaft, which is usually done with three fingers. Needles vary in design from country to country: they may have handles wound with wire (China), cylindrical handles (Japan), handle and shaft in one piece, an especially penetrative design (Korea), or a cylindrical handle soldered or compressed onto the shaft (United States).[11] The *Nei Ching* lists nine traditional types of needles. The most widely used needle in China, the Haochen, is used primarily for puncturing and making surgical incisions, and in massage.

The insertion of an acupuncture needle is a more delicate and difficult procedure than insertion of a hypodermic needle, since acupuncture needles are finer, longer, and not as sharp. Insertion is achieved by placing gentle pressure on the handle while rotating the needle. Owing to the large diameter of many of the Chinese veterinary acupuncture needles and the thickness of the skin of some species, a device known as a needle hammer is sometimes used to place the needle. The acupuncturist inserts the needle into the handle of the hammer and taps it on the skin. Proper technique requires inserting the needles to the correct depth and at the proper angle and applying the appropriate manipulation. To tonify, the needle is rotated clockwise for a short duration, while sedation is accomplished by a counterclockwise rotation of long duration. Insertion of acupuncture needles should be attempted only by individuals who are thoroughly trained in the techniques.[11]

AQUAPUNCTURE

A method frequently used in the horse is aquapuncture, a variation on dry needling. A small-gauge hypodermic needle (usually 25-gauge) is used to inject a small amount (from 0.05–2.0 ml) of a substance at each point. The objective is to stimulate the point with pressure from the injected substance, which usually remains at the site for ten to fifteen minutes.

There are drawbacks to this method. Hypodermic needles are sharper than acupuncture needles and so their use involves a certain amount of tissue damage. Also, although they are somewhat flexible, they cannot be straightened as easily and they can break under stress. Hypodermic needles, however, insert with greater ease and cause less pain than acupuncture needles.

This method is especially effective in horses, who have a muscular component to their skin that enables them to twitch their skin voluntarily in response to local irritation, such as biting flies. Traditional acupuncture needles, which usually are left in place for fifteen minutes to a half-hour, can easily be dislodged by this muscular response in the horse. Aquapuncture is a quick and effective method to achieve similar results. Among the substances commonly used are saline solution, vitamin B-12, DMSO, Serapin, iodine blister, and homeopathic remedies.[2]

ELECTRO-ACUPUNCTURE

A method called electro-acupuncture was developed in China in the 1930s to facilitate treatment of pain and physical ailments and to induce acupuncture analgesia prior to surgery. Electronic devices are applied to increase stimulation of acupuncture points. They are attached either to inserted needles or to damp sponges surrounding an affected area to deliver a current of stimulation through the skin. Another form of electro-acupuncture is achieved with an instrument called an Acuscope. This instrument uses cotton-tipped probes to pass the stimulus through the skin to the underlying nerve structures. Electronic stimulation is more intense than anything achieved by manual manipulation of needles. Its use is essential in acupuncture analgesia for surgery.

Most of the electrostimulators operate on batteries, on A.C. current, and produce a spike wave form. The practitioner can control the frequency, mode, and amplitude of the stimulus. Low-frequency, high-intensity stimulation acts on all three centers—spinal cord, midbrain, and hypothalamus—and the painkilling effect develops slowly but lasts a long time. High-frequency, low-intensity stimulation activates only the midbrain and spinal cord and thus the analgesic effect is quicker but of short duration.

When applying electro-acupuncture to horses, the voltage should be increased gradually until it is determined that the animal feels the stimulus and tolerates it comfortably. Usually, one will see a fasciculation of the muscle. Most horses appear to tolerate it well, but some are very sensitive and become agitated even when the stimulus is mild.[2]

MOXIBUSTION AND HEAT THERAPY

Moxibustion, as described in the *Nei Ching*, is the heating of acupuncture points by burning an herb (moxa) on or above the skin over acupuncture points. This technique is probably as old as acupuncture. *Moxa* is the Chinese name for the powdered leaves of the mugwort *Artemisia vulgaris*, a species of wormwood. Available in stick or cone form, it can be applied directly to the skin or indirectly on a needle. Moxa produces a mild heat that penetrates all meridians, thus it is helpful in eliminating hundreds of diseases.

Moxa acts somehow to enhance the immune system by promoting production of a substance called "complement" that fights infection. This technique is especially effective in problems of chronic pain and with patients who do not respond to needles or herbs.

Another ancient technique employs a hot, sharp-pointed needle like a branding iron that is used to imprint a diagram of cauterization. This technique was used in horses to treat abcesses, skin conditions and severe arthritis. The needle, which is very thick, is heated and inserted through the skin and quickly withdrawn. "Hot Needle" provides stronger stimulation and causes more tissue destruction. This technique is reminiscent of the current practice of firing horses. Other methods using heat are infrared heat lamps, and irritant blister pastes applied to acupuncture points.[7]

LASERPUNCTURE

Low-intensity, or cold, lasers now are being utilized widely in both human and veterinary medicine. They have become very popular with the equine industry as a safe, noninvasive method of promoting wound healing and decreasing the swelling from inflammation. (The term *laser* is an acronym for Light Amplification by Stimulated Emission of Radiation.) Low-intensity lasers use various frequencies and wavelengths to stimulate physiological changes in body cells in order to restore the normal properties of the cells and decrease pain.[2]

Researchers have shown that lasers produce biochemical effects and changes in skin resistance similar to those seen with needling. The use of laser puncture started in 1973 but has not gained acceptance by all veterinary acupuncturists. The two types of lasers most commonly used in acupuncture are the red light emitters (helium-neon gas tube and a laser-simulating diode device), and infrared light emitters (gallium-arsenite diode). The helium-neon lasers have a wavelength of 632–650 nm and penetrate to a depth of 0.8–15 mm. The infrared laser diode has a wavelength of 902 nm generated by a gallium-arsenite diode. It penetrates 10 mm–5 cm (about 2 inches). Infrared lasers come in a great variety of quality and output. The continuous-wave type emits a steady low-power output while the pulsing beam type emits a high-peak output; pain relief is controlled by altering the frequency of pulsation. Infrared lasers are more effective in healing tissues and stimulating acupuncture points, but they require a higher dosage than helium-neon lasers because the beam in the helium-neon laser is concentrated in a much smaller area.

Lasers can be useful to stimulate influential points on the legs of a horse, many of which are difficult to treat with needles. The laser does not have the same energizing effect and balancing action as needles, however. Moxa warms Chi, electro-acupuncture stimulates Chi, while lasers energize Chi. Lasers are best used to enhance the effect of needles and moxa. Laser acupuncture has some obvious merits as a method of stimulation, but it is best viewed as a separate tool rather than a direct replacement for needles.[12]

IMPLANTATION

The Chinese described in ancient texts the implantation of foreign bodies at acupuncture points in order to create severe localized inflammation; the technique provides a more prolonged stimulation of points. Some materials commonly used are gold or stainless steel wire, gold BBs, catgut, and surgical staples. A large-gauge hypodermic needle is used to implant the material. Some conditions in the horse that have been treated successfully with this technique are navicular disease and spavin of the hock.[2]

HEMO-ACUPUNCTURE (BLOOD-LETTING)

This ancient technique uses various types of needles to cut or pierce the skin and blood vessels in order to cause a variable but controlled amount of bleeding. The Chinese literature describes the amount of blood and specific puncture points for certain disease conditions. Because the connective tissue coating the blood vessels is rich in autonomic nerve endings, this technique may induce reflex vasoconstriction or dilatation. Bleeding has not received much popular attention in North America. One condition that still is treated by this technique is laminitis, or founder, where bleeding points are stimulated along the coronary band.[11]

ACUPRESSURE

Acupressure was probably one of the earliest forms of point therapy. The early Chinese physicians describe eight different forms of therapeutic massage. Acupressure is best defined as finger pressure applied to the body surface in a general pattern or at designated points or locations. Several systems utilize external massage, the most common of which is the Japanese system of shiatsu. Veterinarians rarely use acupressure except in conjunction with acupuncture to relieve muscle spasm and pain. It can be taught to nonprofessionals to augment veterinarian-applied acupuncture.[2]

PNEUMO-ACUPUNCTURE (INJECTION OF AIR)

This technique is mentioned in some ancient Chinese prescriptions and is occasionally used today. Air is injected under the skin and massaged downward with the fingers. Coincidentally, this was the treatment of choice for paralysis of the nerves of the shoulder, atrophy of the shoulder muscles, and chronic shoulder problems. Today a similar method is used by some veterinarians in an effort to "free the skin of the shoulder" when shoulder lameness is suspected.[3]

▪ THERAPEUTIC INDICATIONS ▪
IN THE HORSE

Acupuncture is a very powerful type of physiotherapy in which there is controlled activation of the spinal and central nervous system and neuroendocrine and systemic responses. Acupuncture influences the physiological states of the nervous, musculoskeletal, gastrointestinal, urogenital, respiratory, and endocrine systems. It has analgesic, anti-inflammatory, immunostimulant, and immunosuppressant effects. It has antispasmodic effects on the smooth and striated muscles, and influences microcirculation and glandular secretions. Its therapeutic value is to induce homeostasis, or the normal state.[9] The therapeutic effects of acupuncture are possible only when the body is capable of a normal physiological response. Acupuncture has no effect on paralysis due to nerve transection or brain damage, but it does have some effect on peripheral nerve damage. It is ineffective in severe and irreversible pathological changes such as chronic organ damage, fractures, and cartilage degeneration. Acupuncture is not recommended in treating neoplasia (tumors) or severe organic diseases.

The practice of acupuncture should be attempted only by a veterinarian with advanced medical training. In 1974 as a direct result of increasing global interest, the International Veterinary Acupuncture Society (IVAS) came into being, and today its membership includes veterinarians from all parts of the world. This organization conducts postgraduate courses in acupuncture for veterinarians. A list of veterinarians who have completed this course of study is available through the IVAS.

The following sections will discuss some conditions that appear to be very responsive to acupuncture therapy and will explain how acupuncture achieves its effects. The anatomical reference points are shown in the illustration on page 26.

MUSCULOSKELETAL PROBLEMS

Arthritis or osteoarthritis of the knee, hock (spavin), ankle (osselot), or pastern (ringbone) can be defined as the inflammation of any or all components of the joint. Traditionally this condition is treated with systemic anti-inflammatory agents such as phenylbutazone or with local injections of hyaluronic acid or cortisone. Acupuncture alleviates the pain associated with osteoarthritis by stimulating the hypothalamus to release ACTH, which in turn activates the adrenals to release corticosteroids that reduce inflammation. Localized effects at a specific area are achieved by stimulation of local points, which causes a reflex spinal response with inhibition of pain and release of spinal endorphins.

"Sore back" originating in the thoracic, lumbar, or sacral area is a frequent problem in the horse. Of the various treatments for this debilitating condition acupuncture seems to get the best response. The treatments offered by conventional veterinary medicine have not proved satisfactory. They include internal blisters induced with iodine, localized injections with steroids and serapin, and muscle relaxants such as Methocarbacol. It has been postulated that in many cases sore back is due to muscle spasms caused by the overriding and crowding of the dorsal spinous process in the area under the saddle. This author believes that the condition is often secondary, a consequence of the animal altering its gait to compensate for sore hocks or stifles or forelimb lameness. The muscle spasms that appear are a result of disturbed nerve transmission caused by pressure or pinching of the vertebrae due to the altered gait. Western medicine deals with im-

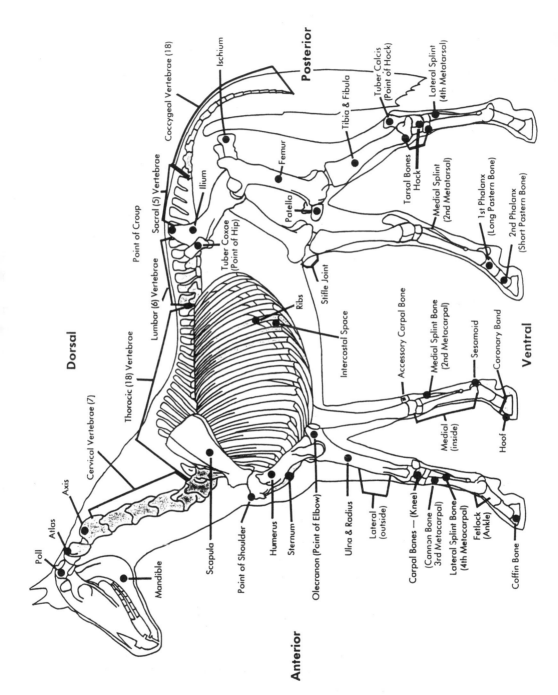

Dorsal

Posterior

Anterior

Ventral

Poll
Atlas
Axis
Cervical Vertebrae (7)
Mandible
Scapula
Point of Shoulder
Humerus
Sternum
Olecranon (Point of Elbow)
Ulna & Radius
Lateral (outside)
Carpal Bones — (Knee)
(Cannon Bone 3rd Metacarpal)
Lateral Splint Bone (4th Metacarpal)
Fetlock (Ankle)
Coffin Bone
Thoracic (18) Vertebrae
Point of Croup
Lumbar (6) Vertebrae
Sacral (5) Vertebrae
Coccygeal Vertebrae (18)
Ilium
Tuber Coxae (Point of Hip)
Ischium
Femur
Patella
Stifle Joint
Ribs
Intercostal Space
Accessory Carpal Bone
Medial Splint Bone (2nd Metacarpal)
Sesamoid
Medial (inside)
Coronary Band
Hoof
Tibia & Fibula
Tuber Calcis (Point of Hock)
Tarsal Bones Hock
Lateral Splint (4th Metatarsal)
Medial Splint (2nd Metatarsal)
1st Phalanx (Long Pastern Bone)
2nd Phalanx (Short Pastern Bone)

paired structures by use of mechanical means or drugs. Acupuncture works by altering the electrical nerve flow, restoring nerve impulses to normal rather than abnormal functioning.[13]

True shoulder lameness apears to be rare. Many horses that are diagnosed with shoulder soreness actually are suffering from bicipital bursitis, which is secondary to a lameness such as navicular disease in the lower portion of the limb. Large Intestine 16 (LI_{16}), an acupressure point that lies near the point of the shoulder, is often mistaken for shoulder soreness. The traditional treatment for soreness in this area is anti-inflammatory agents, local injections, and rest. These measures are not usually very rewarding, however. In contrast, true shoulder lameness from nerve damage and trauma does appear responsive to acupuncture therapy, which utilizes the anti-inflammatory effects of internally produced cortisone to alleviate pain in the joint and to repair nerve and muscle damage.

Laminitis, or founder, is an inflammation of the hoof usually secondary to carbohydrate overload or toxicity. This results in circulatory problems such as congestion, ischemia, and necrosis of the laminae. Traditional therapies include anti-inflammatory agents, antihistamines, and corrective shoeing. Stimulation of acupuncture points releases mast cells from the site, causing the arterioles to enlarge and circulation to the area to increase. Therapeutic bleeding, with large-gauge needles, of specific points along the coronary band also contributes to local alteration in circulation, increasing the blood supply to the hoof.

Navicular disease is the result of altered blood flow to the navicular bone or of secondary osteoarthritis. Acupuncture is frequently successful in alleviating symptoms by increasing the circulation and by releasing the body's own corticosteroids. Pericardium 1 (PC_1) is a good diagnostic point for foot problems such as navicular disease, laminitis, and sole bruises. This point is located behind the elbow under the girth. Many horses that are foot-sore become "girthy" when they are saddled and the girth is tightened; they appear lame or have a shortened forward stride for the first ten to fifteen minutes and then seem to "work out" of the problem.

RESPIRATORY CONDITIONS

Heaves, allergic bronchitis, and chronic bronchiolitis all are synonymous names for a pathological condition of the lungs. The primary symptoms range from coughing and exercise intolerance to respiratory distress. Possible causes are allergies, viral or bacterial infection, and diet. Some common treatments include bronchodilators, expectorants, antibiotics, corticosteroids, and change of housing. Acupuncture appears to have a favorable effect on this condition. Stimulation of therapeutic points causes an increase in the secretion of two neuropeptides, bombesin and VIP (Vaso-active intestinal peptide). Bombesin originates in the cells of the lung and regulates circulation, while VIP is responsible for dilatation of the airway. Other effects seen are an increase of phlegm and mucus with a thinning of their consistency. Soon after treatment the horse may show increased difficulty in breathing, but this soon disappears.

Other respiratory conditions that appear responsive to acupuncture are rhinitis, sinusitis, pharyngitis, and bleeding. Supplemental use of appropriate antibiotics may be necessary to get the best results.

REPRODUCTIVE DISORDERS

The natural breeding season of the horse is during spring and summer. Altering the breeding season to the winter months to produce earlier foals often causes mares to undergo erratic cycling or anaestrus. These problems have been treated successfully by using artificial light to mimic increased daylight hours. This forces the horse to ovulate, as the daylight hours correspond with the amount seen in May—the optimum time of ovulation—and by administering gonadotrophin-releasing hormones, progesterones, and prostaglandins. These techniques do not always work, however. Acupuncture appears to have a beneficial effect in many of these stubborn cases. The most probable explanation for its success is the direct stimulation of the anterior pituitary gland, which controls the secretion of gonadotrophins, follicle-stimulating hormone, luteinizing hormone, and prolactin. Stimulation of the posterior pituitary during delivery can cause a letdown of milk and an increase in uterine contractions.

A stallion that is reluctant to mount a mare, or is not able to complete copulation, may be suffering from a sore back that makes it very painful for him to stand on his hind legs to breed. Stallions with this problem respond remarkably well to acupuncture therapy.

GASTROINTESTINAL PROBLEMS

Gastrointestinal upsets are a common problem in the horse. Conditions such as gaseous colic with increased or decreased motility, impaction, diarrhea, colitis, and ulcers are seen frequently. Some traditional treatments are antispasmodics, anti-inflammatory agents, and tubing with soothing substances such as mineral oil. Acupuncture can be very beneficial not only in alleviating the pain associated with colic but in restoring the gastrointestinal tract to normal functioning. Neuropeptides (VIP, CCK [cholecystokin], insulin, glucagon, gastrin, and somastatin) are located in the intestinal tract and are very receptive to peripheral stimulation of acupuncture points. The body is able to self-regulate these hormones, causing increase or decrease of motility as necessary. Acupuncture also can inhibit or stimulate secretions into the intestinal tract, thereby alleviating diarrhea and constipation. Treatment with acupuncture will not mask any possible surgical condition and is a useful adjunct to conventional colic therapy.

Horses that chew on their stalls ("cribbers") frequently have chronic digestive problems such as mild gastritis and ulcers. Successful treatment of the digestive disorder with acupuncture may result in a disappearance or reduction of cribbing, but the results are temporary.

NEUROLOGICAL PROBLEMS

Peripheral nerve paralysis (radial paralysis), which may be seen following trauma, is very responsive to acupuncture. Points along the course of the affected nerve often are used. In paralysis, electro-acupuncture is usually more effective than needling.

Wobbler syndrome, or cervical ataxia, may be helped by acupuncture. This syndrome is the result of a narrowing or malformation of the cervical vertebrae causing uncoordinated movement, especially an inability to turn sharply and back up. Initial results following several sessions may appear dramatic but long-term results are not very rewarding. Treatment of wobblers is impractical on economic grounds except for valuable bloodstock and pets. Those horses that have similar symptoms as a result of trauma to the neck from falling or being cast have a much more favorable prognosis.

BEHAVIORAL PROBLEMS

Aggressive and nervous behavior frequently is seen in performance horses. Acupuncture appears to have a harmonizing and sedative effect on these animals. Points may be treated with acupressure, needling, or implantation. Massage is the most practical for most horse owners. Some useful points are Bladder 1 (BL_1; medial corner of the eye), Governing Vessel 20 (GV_{20}; top of the head), Triple Heater 17 (TH_{17}; posterior side of the ear), Small Intestine 19 (SI_{19}; lateral to the ear), and Governing Vessel 26 (GV_{26}; at the end of the nasal cartilage).

STIMULATION OF THE IMMUNE SYSTEM

Acupuncture can promote homeostasis by correcting functions of the body that have deviated from normal and by reinforcing the body's own defense mechanisms. Combating diseases with the body's own defense system is indeed the primary role of acupuncture. Laboratory studies show that acupuncture stimulates an increase in serum complement, antibodies, and cortisone, as well as an enhancement of the bactericidal power of plasma. In such conditions as salmonella, acupuncture works not by combating the bacterium itself but by altering the intestinal cells' response to the bacterial toxins. It is most beneficial to the patient when the therapies of Western medicine for the elimination of pathogens are combined with the methods of Eastern medicine for the promotion of self-defense and homeostasis.[14]

Acupuncture has many applications in equine medicine. The success rate in many conditions is above 70 percent, especially in back soreness and in musculoskeletal, reproductive, and respiratory diseases. Acupuncture is often looked upon as a treatment of last resort, however, and therefore many patients live with their problem for years before seeking help. In this case, if success is to be attained it may take several months of treatment. In acute conditions, acupuncture can bring improvement with three to four treatments at weekly or biweekly intervals.

Chronic cases may take months of treatment starting at weekly intervals and continuing with sessions every two to three weeks. To achieve the best results for the horse, acupuncture may be combined with more traditional therapies such as localized joint injection, use of phenylbutazone or other anti-inflammatory, and administration of antibiotics.

Acupuncture is a safe and versatile technique that offers a good alternative to Western veterinary methods for the veterinarian, client, and patient. It cannot cure every condition or every horse, but it has given many a second chance.

▪ DIAGNOSTIC ACUPRESSURE ▪

I have found acupressure diagnosis to be extremely useful in localizing soreness or lameness that is not easily detected with the more traditional techniques of jogging, nerve-blocking, and hoof-testing. Clients are amazed that such a simple procedure—stimulating a few key diagnostic acupuncture points with the fingers—can reveal the source of a problem without the horse stepping out of the stall. The following discussion will present a description of the diagnostic points, so that an owner or trainer can utilize acupuncture diagnosis to locate the source of the horse's problem. Acupuncture diagnosis is not a replacement for veterinary care, but it can be used as an adjunct to the overall care of the horse.

Seeing, hearing, smelling, feeling, and questioning are five diagnostic methods used in traditional Chinese medicine. Acupuncture diagnosis in the horse is best accomplished by applying pressure with the fingers to stimulate specific points along the back called *association*, or *Shu*, points. These points are located on the inner branch of the Bladder meridian about a hand's width lateral to the midline and one *cun* (the width of the sixteenth rib) apart. (See page 34.) Due to anatomic variations in body size and breeds there is some discrepancy in the precise location of certain points. Each point has a direct connection with a meridian and an internal organ.

Alarm, or *Mu*, points are located on the lower portion of the trunk. These points are very important in diagnosis as well as in treatment. Mu points are used together with Shu points for the treatment and diagnosis of acute and chronic disturbances of internal organs. These points can be examined by applying pressure from the fingers or an object such as a needle cap. Whatever tool is used, pressure must be uniform at each point to achieve accurate results. When pain is elicited, the response is a quivering of the muscle, movement away from the pressure, retraction of the back, or sometimes, when a point is very painful, even an attempt to kick or bite. The examination is conducted at two levels: a response to light pressure, or Yang, indicates an acute or superficial condition; a response to deep pressure, or Yin, suggests a chronic situation. Diagnosis starts with the palpation of four key points that are not association points: Bladder 10 (BL_{10}), Small Intestine 16 (SI_{16}), Triple Heater 15 (TH_{15}), and Large Intestine 16 (LI_{16}). (See page 34.)

Bladder 10 (BL_{10}) is located over the wings of the atlas (first vertebra of the neck), behind the poll of the head. This point lies over the occipital nerve. Pain in this area usually indicates soreness in the hind limb on the opposite side. Many horses that appear head-shy or unruly when being fitted with a halter or bridle may be telling you that this point is painful; there may be a problem in a hind limb.

Small Intestine 16 (SI_{16}) is located on the midline between the second and third cervical vertebrae. Its nerve

DIAGNOSTIC POINTS

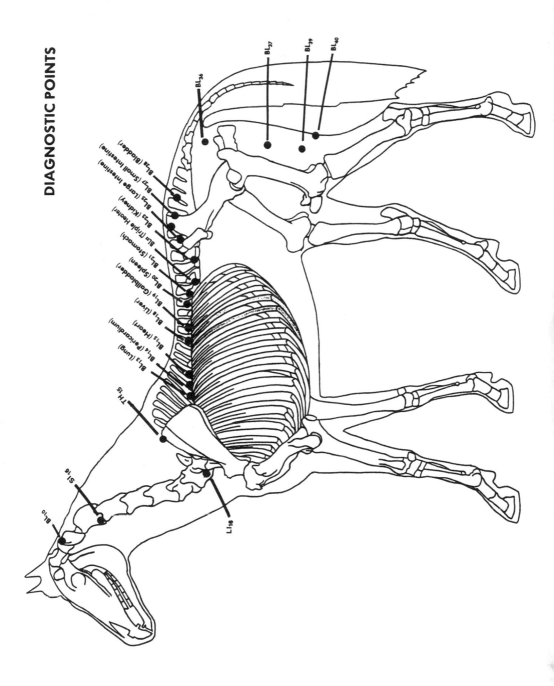

BL₃₆
BL₃₇
BL₃₉
BL₄₀

BL₂₈ (Bladder)
BL₂₇ (Small Intestine)
BL₂₅ (Large Intestine)
BL₂₃ (Kidney)
BL₂₂ (Triple Heater)
BL₂₁ (Stomach)
BL₂₀ (Spleen)
BL₁₉ (Gallbladder)
BL₁₈ (Liver)
BL₁₅ (Heart)
BL₁₄ (Pericardium)
BL₁₃ (Lung)

TH₁₅

ST₁₆

LI₁₆

BL₁₀

supply comes from the cutaneous cervical nerves, which branch to the brachial plexus and phrenic nerve. This meridian travels down the back of the forelimb following the ulnar nerve. Sensitivity at this point may correspond to injury in the superficial flexor tendon, inferior check ligament, shoulder, outside sesamoid, or annular ligament. This point is often tender when there is a subluxation of a cervical vertera or the atlas. Small Intestine 16 (SI_{16}) also relates to sacral injuries on the same or opposite side and to hind-limb lameness. Horses that are very body-sore frequently exhibit pain at this site.

Triple Heater 15 (TH_{15}) is located at the front edge of the scapula at its junction with the scapular cartilage, above the third intercostal space. Its nerve supply comes from the dorsal cervical nerves. The Triple Heater meridian runs up the middle of the outside of the forelimb. Pain at this point may indicate soreness in the suspensory ligament.

Large Intestine 16 (LI_{16}) lies in a depression on the front edge of the scapula two-thirds of the way between Th_{15} and the point of the shoulder. This point lies close to the brachial plexus, which receives its nerve supply from the last three cervical and first two thoracic vertebrae. These nerves branch out to supply the median and axillary nerves on the front of the forelimb. This point has a powerful effect similar to Large Intestine 4 (LI_4) in humans. It affects the sympathetic ganglion, producing endorphine-like effects. Tenderness at this point may be caused by pain in the shoulder, elbow, knee, ankle, shin, and pastern. Sensitivity at points higher up on the meridian corresponds to pain more dorsal on the leg. This point may also relate to hind-limb lameness on the opposite side or to lumbar pain on the same side.

The Association Points are located along the Bladder

meridian, which lies along the back of the trunk. The spinal nerves, which emerge at the head of each intercostal space and run alongside of the vertebral column, correspond to the association points. These nerves supply motor and sensory fibers to the limbs and visceral organs. Activation of the association points is controlled by sympathetic stimulation, which causes enlargement and openings of the sweat and sebaceous glands. Bladders 13–25 are located in the thoracic and lumbar area. Bladders 13, 14, and 15 receive their innervation from the visceral aortic, cardiac, pulmonary, and esophageal branches of the cardiac plexus.

The main source of nerves for Bladders 18–25 is the coeliac plexus, which distributes nerves to the viscera and vessels of the abdominal cavity. The abdominal aortic, gastric, hepatic, and splenic plexuses and the anterior mesenteric plexus arise as unpaired plexuses from the coeliac plexus and supply nerves to their respective organs. The renal, adrenal, spermatic, and utero-ovarian plexuses are paired as they branch out to the organs. These are under the control of the sympathetic nervous system.

Bladder 13 (BL$_{13}$) is the association point for the Lung meridian. The Lung meridian is paired with the Large Intestine meridian and both are related to the element Metal. (See page 38.) Bladder 13 is located below the dorsal spine of the eighth thoracic vertebra, at the caudal edge of the scapular cartilage in the eighth intercostal space. This meridian starts in the lungs and emerges superficially at a level with the third rib at the skin fold of the post-sternal region (LU$_1$). It continues alongside the biceps tendon, then down the anteromedial edge of the radius over the knee and inner splint to the medial sesamoid, ending on the posteromedial aspect of the coronary band (LU$_{11}$). Sensitivity at this point may indicate tenderness inside the front leg on the splint, carpal joint or sesamoid. It is also tender in acute respiratory problems and in cribbing. Lung 1 (LU_1), the alarm point for the Lung meridian, is located between the second and third rib in the intercostal space. Sensitivity at LU_1 and Bladder 13 may indicate deep lung involvement.

Bladder 14 (BL_{14}) is the association point for the Pericardium meridian. (See page 39.) This meridian is paired with the Triple Heater meridian, which is related to the element Fire. Bladder 14 is located below the dorsal spine of the ninth thoracic vertebra in the ninth intercostal space. The Pericardium meridian starts in the lining of the heart and emerges superficially at a point between the fourth rib and the inside of the elbow (PC_1). From there it courses along the medial side of the biceps and down the inside of the front leg over the chestnut, knee and tendon to a point between the bulbs of the heel (PC_9). Bladder 14 may show tenderness in the presence of anxiety, nervousness, or behavioral disorders. It may also be indicative of cardiac pain or stuffiness in the chest.

Pericardium 1 (PC_1) appears to be a good diagnostic point for conditions of the foot such as founder or navicular disease. Conception Vessel 17 (CV_{17}) is the alarm point for the Pericardium meridian; it is located along the midline at a level with the caudal border of the elbow in the fourth intercostal space.

Bladder 15 (BL_{15}), the association point for the Heart meridian, is located in the tenth intercostal space. (See page 40.) The Heart and Small Intestine meridians are paired and related to the element Fire. The Heart meridian initially arises from the heart but starts superficially in the center of the axilla (HT_1). It then travels down the posteromedial side of the arm to the back of the knee. The meridian then crosses from behind the knee to the outside of the forelimb where it continues along the posterior aspect, ending at a point on the posterior lateral aspect of

LUNG MERIDIAN (BL₁₃)

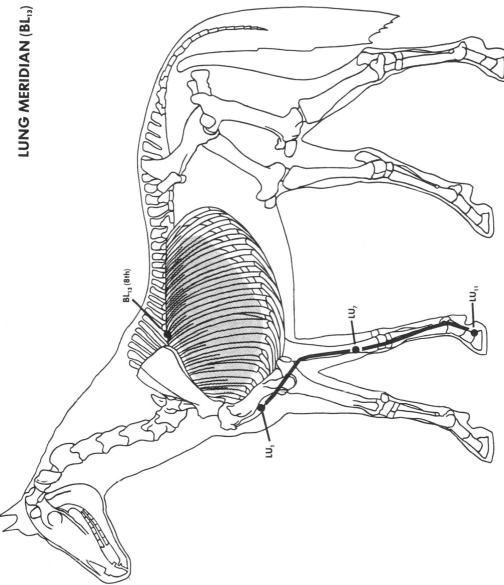

BL₁₃ (8th)

LU₇

LU₁₁

LU₁

PERICARDIUM (BL₁₄)

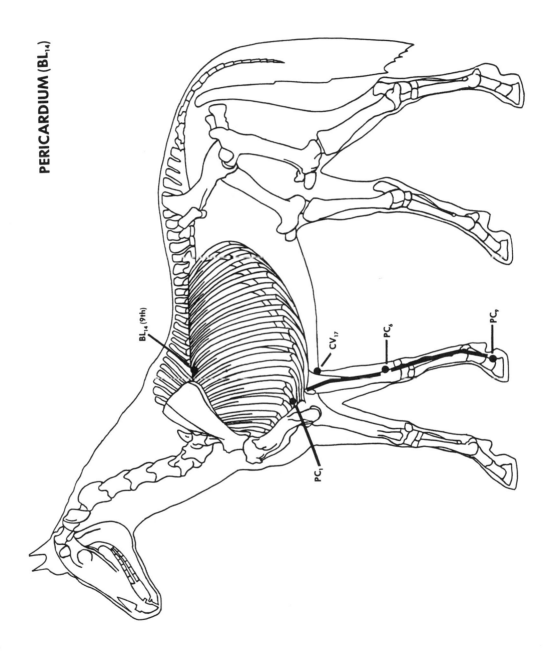

BL₁₄ (9th)

CV₁₇

PC₆

PC₉

PC₁

HEART MERIDIAN (BL₁₅)

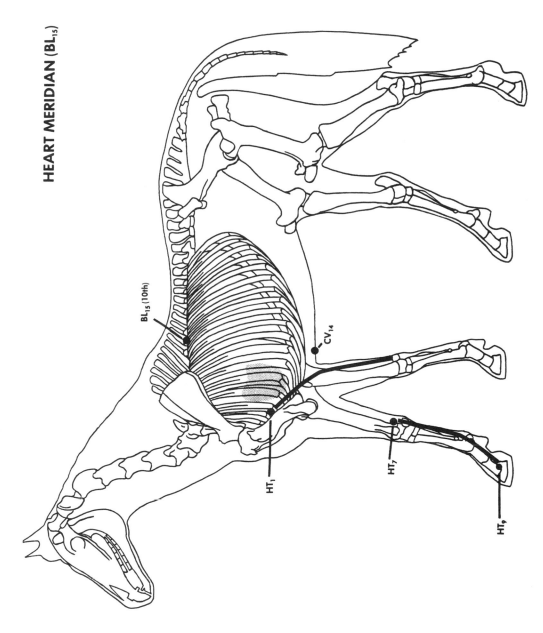

the coronary band (HT_9). Bladder 15 may be tender in problems toward the back of the forelimb such as tendons and sesamoids. Sensitivity here is also concomitant with anxiety, nervousness, and circulatory problems. Conception Vessel (CV_{14}) is the alarm point for the Heart meridian. It is located on the midline of the abdomen about the level of the xiphoid.

Bladder 16 (BL_{16}) is the association point for the Governing Vessel meridian and is found below the top of the spine of the eleventh thoracic vertebra. (See page 42.) This is an extra meridian and is not paired. It runs along the midline of the back, starting at a point between the anus and the root of the tail (GV_1). It then continues along the back over the lumbosacral space (Bai Hui) to the top of the head (GV_{20}), down to a point midway between the lower limit of the nostrils (GV_{26}), and finally to its endpoint between the lip and the upper gum (GV_{28}). Bladder 16 is used to increase or reduce Governing Vessel activity, which controls the supraspinous ligament running along the neck from the poll to the tip of the withers. Problems of this ligament are common in horses that are stall-bound and seldom allowed the opportunity to fully stretch their neck and back muscles while drinking from streams, rolling, and grazing. Weakness of the supraspinous and nuchal ligaments make the horse prone to neck and back problems and to tenderness of the bursa at the point of the withers. An imbalance in this meridian can indicate stiffness and pain anywhere in the spinal column.

For therapeutic purposes, there are several points along this meridian that can be stimulated easily with acupressure. GV_{20}, located at the point of the head, is an excellent calming point for horses. Massaging GV_1 (above the anus) and CV_1 (below the anus) may stimulate initial defecation in foals. A useful shock point in emergencies in all species is GV_{26}, located between the nostrils. Not only does this point stimulate respiration and circulation in newborn

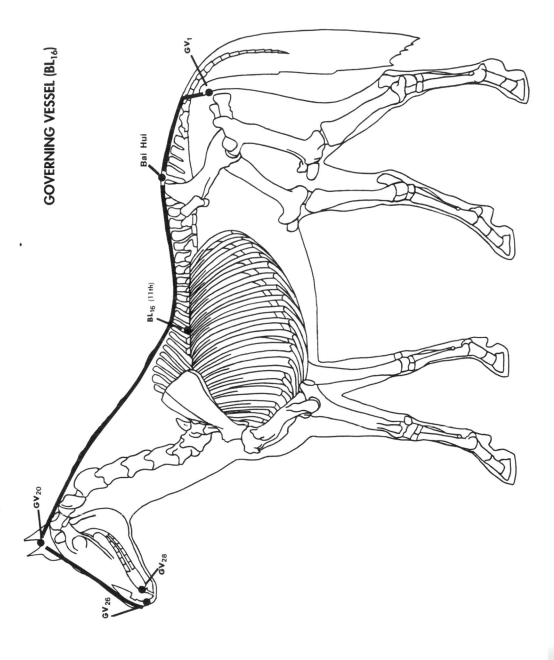

GOVERNING VESSEL (BL₁₆)

foals, this is the point routinely stimulated when a twitch is applied for restraint. Pressure on this point releases endorphins, which create a euphoric sensation in the horse. The tip of the tail (GV_0) is used in horses that are unable to stand or are unconscious. This point can be stimulated by pinching or with a laser.

Bladder 17 (BL_{17}) is the association point for the Diaphragm and is located in the twelfth intercostal space. (See page 44.) This point is not associated with a specific meridian. It appears painful when there is a change in blood composition such as in anemia, dehydration, focal infections, and toxic poisoning. This point is useful in treating anemia, increasing hemoglobin and PCV (packed cell volume), reducing blood pressure in the lung vessels of bleeders, and increasing clotting time. It is also useful with GV_{26} for stimulating respiration in newborn foals and as an immunostimulant point in viral diseases.

Bladder 18 (BL_{18}) is the Shu point for the Liver meridian and is located in the fourteenth intercostal space. (See page 45.) It is found above Spleen 21, which appears as a distinct depression on the side of the chest. The Liver and Gall Bladder meridians are related to the element Wood. This meridian starts on the anteriomedial aspect of the coronary band of the hind leg (LIV_1) and courses up the inside of the hind limb over the pastern, sesamoid, and splint to the inside front of the hock. It continues from there to the inner thigh, to the inside of the hip joint, and ends in the fourteenth intercostal space at the level of the elbow (LIV_{14}). The internal branches go to the liver, eyes, and "gall bladder function." Liver 14 is the alarm point for the Liver meridian and is sensitive when there is an increase in liver enzymes from either liver disease or muscle damage, from tying-up. "Tying-up" is the clinical symptom of muscle cramping and stiff gait. This may be caused by an alteration of blood supply to the muscles.

DIAPHRAGM (BL$_{17}$)

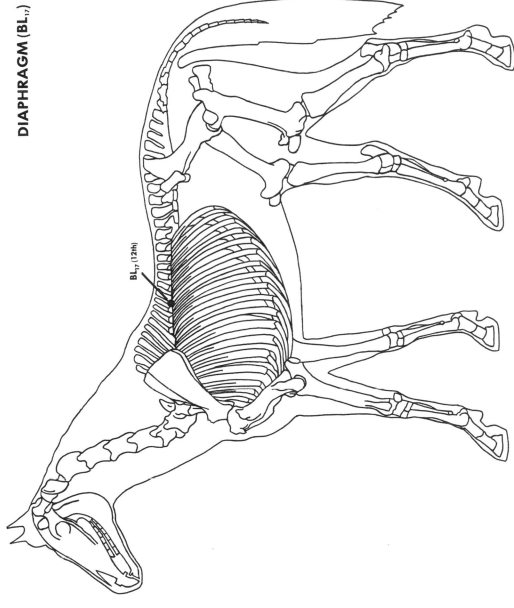

BL$_{17}$ (12th)

LIVER MERIDIAN (BL₁₈)

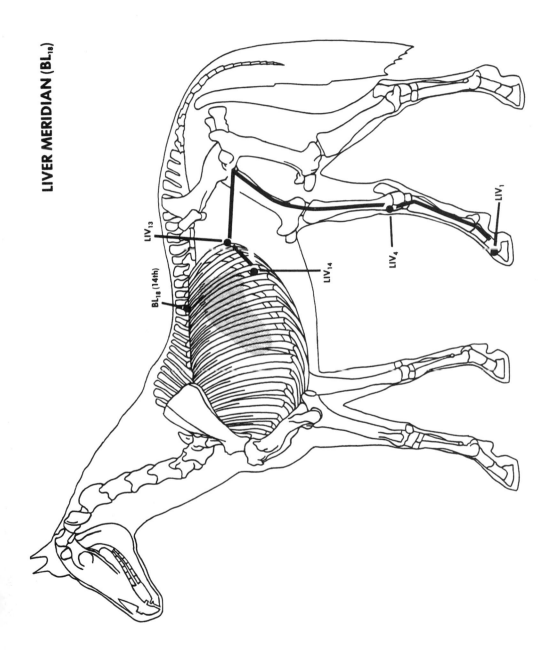

The Liver meridian controls the tendons, joints, and muscles and dominates the movement of the limbs. It is used to treat inflammation of the muscles (myositis), tying-up, and elevation of the liver enzymes SGOT and CPK. Pain at Bladder 18 is seen more frequently than pain at other points since the skeletal system of the horse is 70 percent muscle. It is often painful in racehorses that are undergoing heavy training. Usually Bladder 18 is most sensitive on the side opposite the inciting problem, because the horse usually twists its body to compensate for the pain. The Liver meridian in traditional Chinese medicine controls the eye, so Bladder 18 may be tender as a concomitant of eye problems such as conjunctivitis and tearing. This association point may also be tender in connection with allergies, since the Liver meridian controls the immunoregulators serum albumin and globulin.

The Gall Bladder meridian is one of the most frequently used meridians in the horse. *Bladder 19* (BL_{19}) is the association point for the Gall Bladder meridian and is located in the fifteenth intercostal space. (See page 47.) The Gall Bladder and Liver meridians are paired and are related to the element Wood. The Gall Bladder meridian begins at the outside corner of the eye (GB_1), then runs to the ear and over the head to the occipital condyle (GB_{20}). From here the meridian follows the upper edge of the neck to the front of the scapula, across the chest to the fifteenth intercostal space, slightly dorsal to Liver 14 (GB_{24}, alarm point for the Gall Bladder meridian). From here it courses to the back edge of the eighteenth rib (GB_{25}). The meridian then curves around the hip joint and down the outside of the thigh and stifle, down the leg over the splint, and over the ankle, ending on the anterolateral aspect of the coronary band (GB_{44}). Internal branches go to the liver and "gall bladder function." The horse lacks a gall bladder, but this meridian has other important local uses. Bladder 19 is associated with the hip, outside stifle, outside hock,

GALLBLADDER MERIDIAN (BL₁₉)

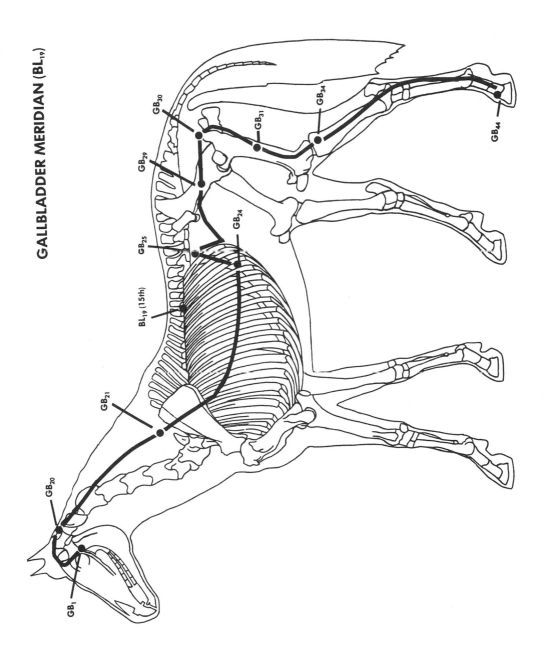

splint, and curb. Many horses develop lameness in the hip area of the hind limb as a result of sciatica and spasms in the superficial gluteal muscles. This condition may result from the horse shifting its weight to compensate for a forelimb lameness, chronic soreness in the hock or stifle, or primary sciatica from lumbosacral problems. Bladder 19 may also be tender in connection with muscular problems such as tying-up syndrome and elevated liver enzymes. Soreness in the tendons and ligaments may also cause reactivity.

Bladder 20 (BL_{20}) is the association point for the Spleen meridian and is located in the last intercostal space. (See page 49.) The Spleen and Stomach meridians are paired and associated with the element Earth. The meridian starts on the posteriomedial aspect of the coronary band (SP_1) on the hind limb and travels up the inner aspect of the hind limb over the pastern and splint, to the hock and stifle. It then curves along the side of the chest to the fourth intercostal space (SP_{20}). The meridian then turns posteriorly and ends in the fourteenth intercostal space (SP_{21}). Spleen 21 can be felt as a large hole in the center of the chest. This point is considered the controller of all Yin meridians. Spleen 21 is also useful in finding Bladder 18, which is located directly above it. The internal branches go to the spleen-pancreas, the stomach, and the muscles.

In Chinese medicine the "spleen" is associated with control of the blood and domination of the muscles and limbs. Bladder 20 may be tender in "bleeders" and horses with other blood and circulation disorders. Pain is also evident in digestive disorders such as impaction, colic, and diarrhea, and in functional disorders of the spleen and pancreas. Sensitivity occurs with lameness of the inside stifle and hock (cunean tendon) and with thoracolumbar injury. Spleen 20 is a diagnostic point for pain of the knee.

Liver 13 is the alarm point for the Spleen meridian and is found on the tip of the eighteenth rib. Livers 13 and 14

SPLEEN MERIDIAN (BL₂₀)

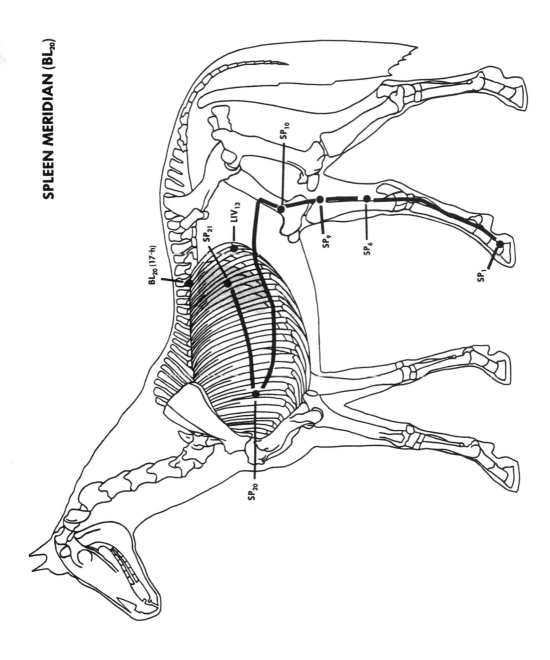

SP₁₀

LIV₁₃

SP₂₁

BL₂₀ (17-h)

SP₉

SP₆

SP₁

SP₂₀

frequently are sensitive when a horse is very muscle-sore. They are used therapeutically to lower the muscle enzymes.

Bladder 21 (BL_{21}) is the association point for the Stomach meridian and is found behind the last rib (T_{18}) at the thoracolumbar junction. (See page 51.) The Stomach and Spleen meridians are paired and relate to the element Earth. The Stomach meridian begins below the eye (ST_1) and runs through the mouth and over the joint between the upper and lower jaws. It then courses along the lower edge of the neck to a point in front of the shoulder, then down the lower abdomen parallel to the midline. From here the meridian runs to the groin toward the hip and over the lateral side of the thigh and stifle. Continuing down the leg, it crosses over the front of the hock and runs down the leg to the anterior aspect of the coronary band (ST_{45}). Internal branches go to the stomach, spleen, and pancreas.

Bladder 21 may be tender in digestive disorders, impaction, colic, lack of appetite, and weight loss. Sensitivity can also be found in horses with infected or sharp teeth. Discomfort caused by colic can be alleviated by massaging ST_2 (which is located in a depression below the inside corner of the eye) and ST_{36} (on the tibial crest). The Stomach meridian relates to the anterolateral hind-limb lameness, stifle lameness, thoracolumbar injury, and pain in the sacrosciatic ligament. Soreness in the stifle area can be confirmed by finding concurrent sensitivity at Bladder 21 and at Bladders 36 and 37 (these points are found in the crease between the biceps femoris and semitendinosus). Stomach 10, found one hand (4 inches) in front of the point of the shoulder, relates to the stifle on the same side and may also be used as a diagnostic point.

Conception Vessel 12 is the alarm point for the Stomach meridian and is located on the midline of the abdomen halfway between the xiphoid and the navel. This point is

STOMACH MERIDIAN (BL$_{21}$)

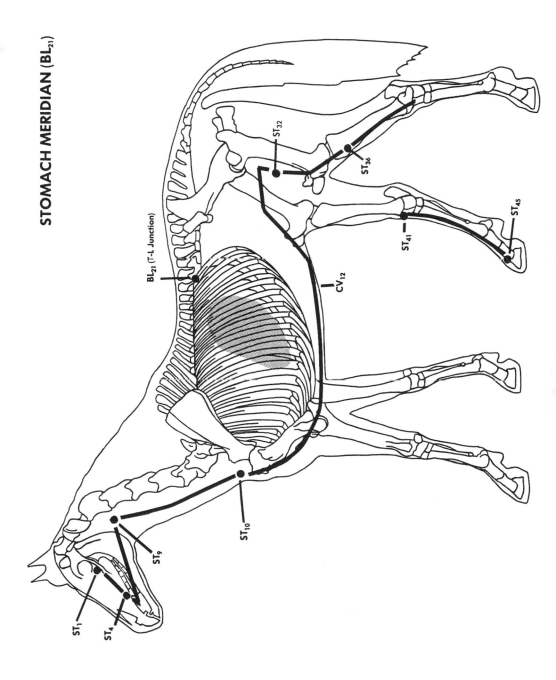

ST$_{32}$

ST$_{36}$

ST$_{45}$

ST$_{41}$

BL$_{21}$ (T-L Junction)

CV$_{12}$

ST$_{10}$

ST$_9$

ST$_1$

ST$_4$

often painful in colic or stomach ulcers. CV_{12} is frequently tender in cribbers, as it has been suggested that this vice may be the result of irritation of the stomach.

Bladder 22 (BL_{22}) is the association point for the Triple Heater meridian and is located on the Bladder meridian at the level of the first and second lumbar vertebrae. (See page 53.) This meridian is paired with the Pericardium meridian and relates to the element Fire. The Triple Heater meridian starts at a point on the front of the coronary band of the forelimb (TH_1) and runs up the anterolateral aspect of the leg over the cannon bone, knee, radius, and elbow, finally up to a point behind the shoulder joint (TH_{14}). This is a local diagnostic point for shoulder lameness. From this point the meridian courses over the front of the scapula, up the middle of the neck to a point below the back of the ear (TH_{17}), over the root of the ear, ending above the outside corner of the eye (TH_{23}). Internal branches go to the Pericardium and endocrine centers.

The Triple Heater meridian is an important point in hormonal-endocrine imbalances of the thyroid, adrenals, and gonads, relating especially to infertility in stallions and mares. TH_{16} is located over the third and fourth cervical vertebrae and is a good diagnostic point in mares for ovarian pain from cysts or ovulation, and in stallions for testicular pain from inguinal-ring problems and cryptorchidism. Mares are more sensitive on the left side, while colts are more sensitive on the right side. Pain from this point can cause muscle spasms in the neck and create a choppy forward stride in the limb. Bladder 22 may be tender in disorders of body-heat regulation (such as seen with nonsweaters), pain in the cervical vertebrae, soreness along the outside of the forelimb, and thoracolumbar problems.

Conception Vessel 5 is the alarm point for the Triple Heater meridian and is found on the midline of the abdomen halfway between the symphysis of the pubis and

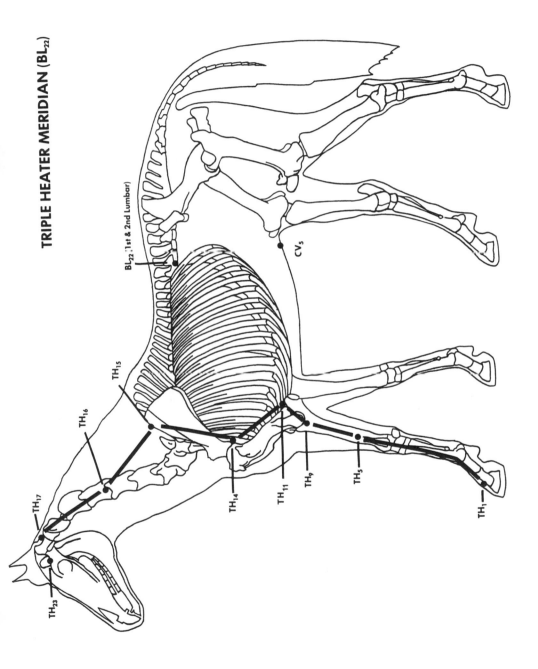

TRIPLE HEATER MERIDIAN (BL₂₂)

the umbilicus. This point is also diagnostic for breeding problems and thyroid disorders and may be massaged for therapeutic effect.

Bladder 23 (BL$_{23}$) is the association point for the Kidney meridian and is found on the Bladder meridian below the second and third lumbar vertebrae straight above the end of the last rib. (See page 55.) The Kidney and Bladder meridians are paired and relate to the element Water. The Kidney meridian begins between the bulbs of the heel on the hind leg (KI$_1$) and courses up the posteromedial aspect of the cannon bone, hock, and stifle to the inner thigh. From here it runs along the lower abdomen (three fingers to the side of the midline), to the inside of the muscles of the forelimb. It ends in the first intercostal space at the sternum (KI$_{27}$). Internal branches go to the kidney, bones, ear, spinal cord, adrenals, ovaries, and bladder.

Bladder 23 may be tender in urinary, adrenal, and fertility disorders and when there is pain in the thoracolumbar area. This point relates to the inside of the hind limb and, in conjunction with Bladder 39, is a reliable diagnostic point for pain in the hock area. Bladder 39 is located in a hole at the end of the groove between the semitendinosus and biceps femoris. This is the point where the common peroneal nerve and tibial nerve branch to serve both the inside and outside of the hock joint.

Gallbladder 25 (GB$_{25}$) is the alarm point for the Kidney meridian and is located behind the costo-chondral junction of the eighteenth rib and the lumbar muscles. In traditional Chinese medicine, the "kidney" stores both Congenital and Acquired Chi. The Yin and Yang of the Kidney meridian nourish and warm the internal organs and thus any imbalance in the "kidney" will be detected by pain by Gallbladder 25, indicating some internal disturbance.

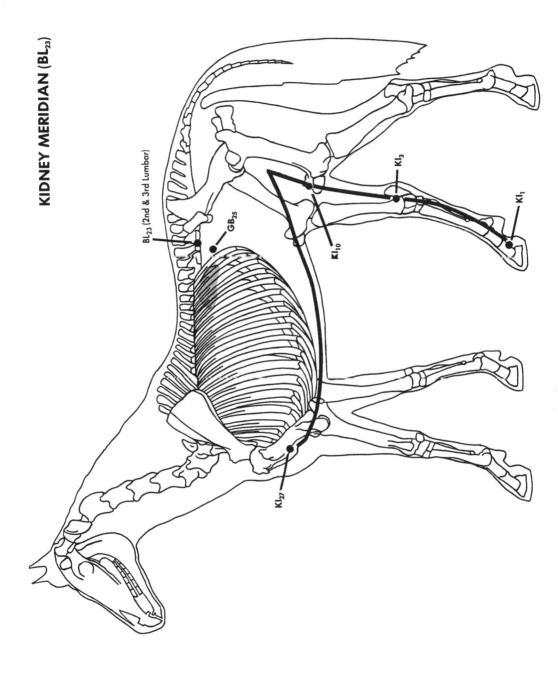

KIDNEY MERIDIAN (BL₂₃)

*   *   *

Bladder 24 (BL$_{24}$) is located one *cun* (the width of the sixteenth rib) behind Bladder 23 and is called the Sea of Energy. (See page 57.) This point is not used for diagnosis but mainly for its local effects in treating pain in the lumbosacral area.

Bladder 25 (BL$_{25}$) is the association point for the Large Intestine meridian and is located between the fifth and sixth lumbar vertebrae at the anterior edge of the wings of the ilium, near the origin of the middle gluteal muscle. (See page 58.) The Large Intestine and Lung meridians are coupled and related to the element Metal. This meridian starts at the anteromedial aspect of the coronary band of the forelimb (LI$_1$) and then ascends up the inside of the pastern, fetlock, and splint. It then crosses over the front of the knee and continues laterally up the forearm to the elbow and shoulder, up the ventral area of the neck, over the larynx and lower jaw, and ending beside the nostril (LI$_{20}$). Internal branches go to the colon and lung.

Sensitivity at Bladder 25 may indicate a problem in the opposite forelimb, which would be confirmed by simultaneous pain at LI$_{16}$ on the opposite forelimb. Tenderness is also seen with problems of the sacroiliac and iliolumbar ligaments and with pain in the middle gluteal muscle. Intestinal disorders such as colic and impaction may also create sensitivity at this point. Large Intestine 4 is a master point and very useful for many conditions in humans and small animals. In the horse, however, the exact location of this point is questionable due to the loss of digits on the forelimb through evolution. Large Intestine 16, located on the front edge of the scapula, appears to have similar effects.

The alarm point for the Large Intestine meridian is Stomach 25, located on the lower abdomen to the side of the navel. This is a reliable diagnostic point to detect ulcers.

SEA OF ENERGY (BL₂₄)

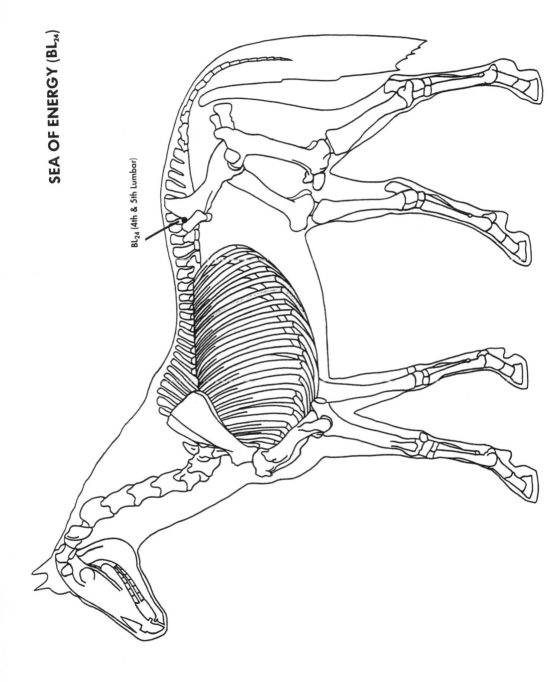

BL₂₄ (4th & 5th Lumbar)

LARGE INTESTINE (BL₂₅)

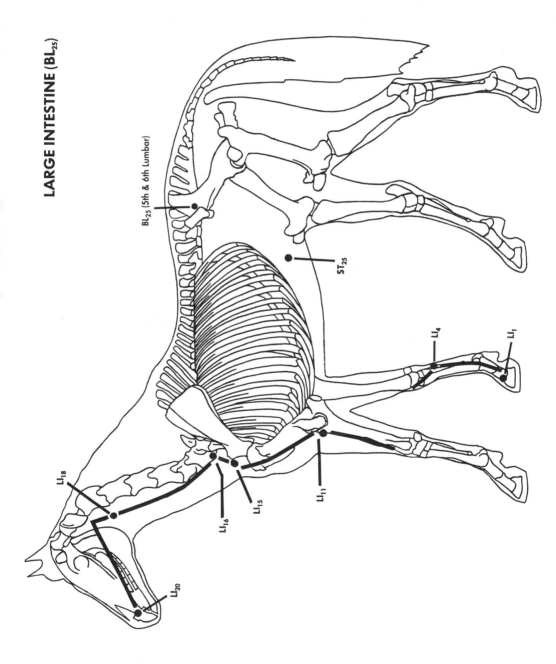

BL₂₅ (5th & 6th Lumbar)

ST₂₅

LI₄

LI₁

LI₁₈

LI₁₆

LI₁₅

LI₁₁

LI₂₀

The nerve supply for the lumbosacral Shu points comes from the pelvic part of the sympathetic trunk, which begins at the last lumbar vertebra and extends along the pelvic surface of the sacrum. The sacral ganglia supply nerves to the rectum, bladder, uterus, and penis. The location of these nerves coincides closely with Bladders 26, 27 and 28. These points are under the control of the parasympathetic nervous system.

Bladder 26 (BL₂₆) is called the Gates of Origin and is located one *cun* behind Bladder 25. (See page 60.) This point is not diagnostic for any meridian, but it appears active in local conditions of the lumbar and sacral area.

Bladder 27 (BL₂₇) is the association point for the Small Intestine meridian and is located on the Bladder meridian below the foramen between the first and second sacral vertebrae. (See page 61.) The Heart and Small Intestine meridians are paired and related to the element Fire. The Small Intestine meridian starts on the anterolateral aspect of the coronary band of the foreleg (SI₁), continues dorsally over the sesamoid, splint, knee, and elbow, then over the triceps muscle and up the scapula. From here the meridian continues over the cervical spine and ends at a depression on the side of the ear (SI₁₉). Internal branches go to the small intestine and heart.

This point may be tender in problems of the back side of the forelimb involving the tendons, check ligaments (superior and inferior), and sesamoids (at each ankle bone). Sensitivity may also be seen with sacrococcygeal and sacral plexus injury, pain in the biceps femoris, and intestinal dysfunction. Small Intestine 19, which is located in a depression on the side of the ear, is a good tranquilizing point. Small Intestine 9, found below the shoulder in a hole between the muscle bellies of the triceps, is a good diagnostic point for shoulder lameness.

Conception Vessel 4 is the alarm point for the Small

GATES OF ORIGIN (BL$_{26}$)

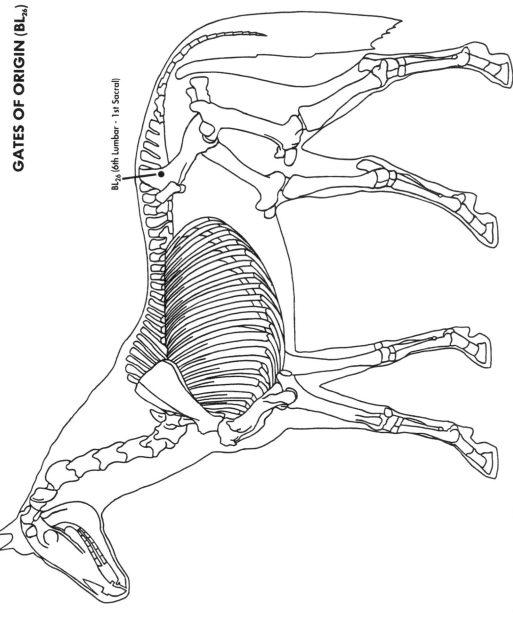

BL$_{26}$ (6th Lumbar - 1st Sacral)

SMALL INTESTINE (BL₂₇)

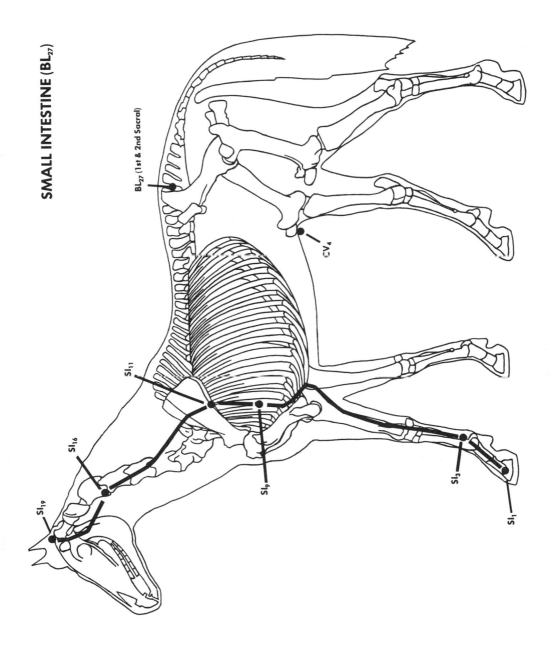

Intestine meridian and is found three *Cun* below the umbilicus on the midline of the abdomen.

Bladder 28 (BL$_{28}$) is the association point for the Bladder meridian and is located on the Bladder meridian below the foramen between the second and third sacral vertebrae. (See page 63.) The Bladder and Kidney meridians are paired and are associated with the element Water. The Bladder meridian starts at the inside corner of the eye (BL$_1$), continues over the head inside the ears to the wing of the atlas (BL$_{10}$). From here it runs down the neck and along the upper edge of the scapula. Here the meridian splits into two branches, which both run parallel to the spine from the third thoracic to the fourth sacral vertebra. Corresponding points on the inner and outer branches lie in the same intercostal space and are functional pairs. Both branches continue down the hind leg. The inner branch runs in the groove between the biceps femoris and the semitendinosus. The outer branch is about three inches anterior to this. The branches join behind the stifle and run to the outside of the hock, splint, and sesamoid and ends on the posterolateral aspect of the coronary band (BL$_{67}$). Internal branches go to the kidney, bladder, and pelvic functions.

The Bladder meridian is the most important of all the meridians, not only diagnostically but also therapeutically. All the association points are located on this channel, and points on this meridian are used in almost every acupuncture prescription.

Bladder 28 may be tender in urogenital disorders such as with endometritis and vaginal inflammation due to windsucking. Mares who are tender at this point may respond favorably to a Caslick's procedure, the sewing together of the edges of the vulva to prevent infection.

Bladder 28 is an important point in all disorders of the spinal column, from the atlas to the sacrum. Common problems that activate this point are cervical misalign-

BLADDER MERIDIAN (BL₂₈)

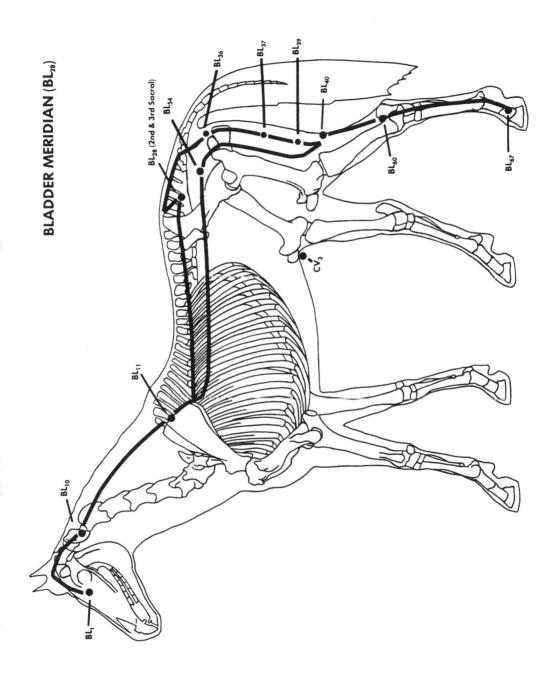

BL₃₆

BL₃₇

BL₃₉

BL₄₀

BL₅₄

BL₂₈ (2nd & 3rd Sacral)

BL₆₀

BL₆₇

CV₃

BL₁₁

BL₁₀

BL₁

ment, sacrococcygeal injury, and strain in the semimem-branosus and tendinosus muscles. This meridian also relates to any problems along its course on the outside of the hind limb.

Conception Vessel 3 is about four *cun* below the umbilicus on the midline of the abdomen and is the alarm point for the Bladder meridian.

• CONCLUSION •

Sensitivity is never seen when examining a healthy horse, superficial wounds, joints that have been injected with corticosteroids or hyaluronic acid, or within the first three to four days of an acute disease. Pain at the diagnostic points does not appear to be diminished by administration of anti-inflammatory agents such as phenylbutazone or Banamine. This fact makes diagnosis by acupressure useful in examining horses on medication that may appear sound when exercised but actually have an underlying lameness.

Frequently, many association points appear tender simultaneously. Varying the pressure at each point may help to determine which point is the most sensitive. The technique requires patience and practice, but it can be very helpful to the horse owner or trainer in localizing affected areas. This technique is not to be a substitute for proper veterinary care; when any lameness appears a veterinarian should be consulted. Acupressure diagnosis is an ancient tool that can be an invaluable aid in modern times.

CONCEPTION VESSEL

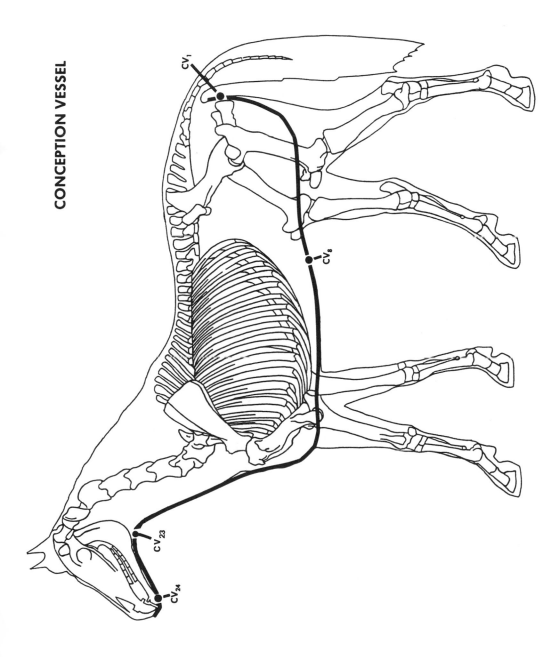

▪ NOTES ▪

1. "A.V.M.A. Policy Statements and Guidelines." *A.V.M.A. Directory.* 1991.

2. Altman, S. *Acupuncture Therapy in Small Animal Practice. Textbook of Veterinary Internal Medicine.* Vol. 1. Philadelphia: W. B. Saunders, 1989.

3. Klide, A. *Veterinary Acupuncture.* Philadelphia: University of Pennsylvania Press, 1977.

4. American Journal of Acupuncture, Vol. 6, No. 2, 1978.

5. International Veterinary Acupuncture Society. Brochure.

6. Altman, S. *An Introduction to Acupuncture for Animals.* 1981.

7. Xinnong, C. *Chinese Acupuncture and Moxibustion.* Beijing: Foreign Language Press, 1987.

8. American Journal of Acupuncture, Vol. 9. No. 2, 1981.

9. Rogers, P., and M. Cain. *Clinical Acupuncture in the Horse.* Proceedings of the Thirteenth International Congress on Veterinary Acupuncture. Belgium: Belgium Acupuncture Society, 1987.

10. Stux, G., and B. Pomeranz. *Acupuncture Textbook and Atlas.* Berlin-Heidelberg and New York: Springer-Verlag, 1987.

11. Klide, A. *Science and Techniques of Veterinary Acupuncture.* Proceedings of the Fiftieth Annual American Animal Hospital Association, 1983.

12. Harrison, T. "Laser Acupuncture: Can Lasers Replace Needles? A Review of Current Literature." *AJA*, Vol. 17, No. 4, 1989.

13. Loo, C. "Symptoms Associated with Impaired Transmission of Nerve Impulses." *AJA*, Vol. 13, No. 4, 1985, pp. 319–330.

14. Dinzong, W. "Acupuncture Promotes Body Self-Defense." *AJA*, Vol. 14, No. 4, 1986, pp. 123–126.

Special thanks to my family: Barry, Alexis, and Brooke Snader.
Charts by Franklin Graphics (Malvern, Pennsylvania 19355).

Note: For a list of certified veterinarians in your area contact International Veterinary Acupuncture Society, 2140 Conestoga Road, Chester Springs, PA 19425.

CHIROPRACTIC

SHARON L. WILLOUGHBY, D.V.M., D.C.

INTRODUCTION

At every horse show and athletic competition, there are many horses working below their potentials due to pain and stiffness. Considerable time and money is spent pursuing the causes of and solutions to decreased equine performance. Owners and trainers administer medications such as painkillers and muscle relaxants, add dietary supplements, try new equipment such as "orthopedic" saddle pads, and stall-rest horses for extended periods. Sometimes these methods solve the problems. Frequently, however, the symptoms are only alleviated for temporary relief. The horse returns to work with the same restrictions and problems.

The unrecognized cause of pain and stiffness in these horses may be problems in the spinal column. Subluxations, or misalignments of the bones in the spine, may cause decreased flexibility, lack of muscle function, or even problems in the nervous system. Chiropractic techniques offer a unique solution for many of the health and performance problems of horses by restoring the function of the back and neck.

The following list describes several typical equine problems. In each case, the horse responded favorably to chiropractic care.

- Swedish Warmblood used in third/fourth-level dressage resists engagement of rear quarters by not flexing properly at the lumbosacral junction.

- Quarter Horse used as barrel racer has increasing difficulty bending the back to the right around the first barrel.

- Thoroughbred used as hunter/jumper is stiff in low back and cannot "open up" or extend the back during jumping.

- Five-gaited Saddlebred has difficulty with rack as result of fixation in sacroiliac joint.

- Standardbred pacer continually bears out when racing due to pelvic rotation.

- Arabian used in show pleasure class repeatedly clenches teeth in pain as it attempts to bend and flex stiff midback.

- Polo horse fights bit and resists flexing head due to problem in temporomandibular (jaw) joint.

- Thoroughbred racehorse with back pain runs with head held too high and decreased length of stride.

- Hanoverian used in combined training cannot flex at poll due to problem with atlas (first cervical vertebra).

• Yearling Quarter Horse filly injured in trailer accident is unable to lift head due to misalignment of cervical vertebrae.

Chiropractic has been a successful health-care approach for the human patient for over one hundred years. Although many chiropractors have applied this practice to animals, only recently has there been considerable study of the application of spinal manipulation to horses. Chiropractic does not replace traditional veterinary medicine, but it can be used as part of the total health-care plan for the horse.

Chiropractic manipulation should be practiced only by a professional—either a chiropractor or veterinarian— who has had advanced training in the techniques. There are, however, several simple techniques, which are explained in this chapter, that can be used by the horse owner to examine and care for the back and neck of the horse. This chapter is also designed to provide an understanding of the basics of chiropractic care so that the horse owner will recognize when the services of an equine chiropractor are needed.

• WHAT IS CHIROPRACTIC? •

Chiropractic is defined by one chiropractic authority, A. E. Homewood, as "that science and art which utilizes the inherent recuperative powers of the body, and deals with the relationship between the nervous system and the spinal column, including its immediate articulations and the role of this relationship in the restoration and maintenance of health." A basic premise of chiropractic, then, is that the animal's body has the inborn ability to maintain health. This ability of the body to heal itself is mediated by the nervous system. When the nervous system is functioning properly, the tissues of the body can respond normally in fighting disease and in repairing damaged tissues. A chiropractic adjustment or manipulation restores the function of the spinal column by restoring the function of the nervous system.

Chiropractic care is a drugless, noninvasive approach that offers many benefits for the health and performance of the horse. An examination before the adjustment will identify the problems of the spinal column that are present and in need of correction. Adjustments are made directly on misaligned vertebrae. Jerking on legs or tails is not a chiropractic adjustment. The chiropractor performs an adjustment by applying controlled forces to the long processes that extend off the bones of the spine. Simply because horses are large does not mean that powerful forces are needed to adjust their vertebrae. The joints of the spine are movable and if the correct angle is used, the adjustment is relatively easy and of low force. The length of the vertebral processes gives the adjuster the mechanical advantage of leverage. The chiropractor can produce effective adjustments of the horse's spine by using only his or her hands.

▪ THE SPINAL COLUMN ▪

The spinal column of the horse is a complex structure consisting of bones, nerves, ligaments, muscles, and blood vessels. The small bones that make up the spinal column are called vertebrae. Excluding the tail, there are usually thirty-two vertebrae in the spinal column of the horse. (See page 26.) The seven bones of the neck are called cervical vertebrae. Eighteen thoracic vertebrae make up the region of the withers and upper back. The lower back of the horse has six lumbar vertebrae. The sacrum consists of five fused segments; it joins the vertebral column to the pelvis. The tail of the horse is made up of sixteen to eighteen modified vertebrae called coccygeals. There can be variations in the number of vertebrae. The Arabian horse, for example, may have only five lumbar vertebrae and sometimes only seventeen thoracic vertebrae.

The vertebrae can be traced along the neck and back by palpating the bony projections, or processes, that extend from each vertebra; the cervical vertebrae in the lower one-third of the neck are easily palpated. These projections are quite long in certain sections of the spine, such as the upper thoracic (withers) region. The central portions of these thoracic and lumbar vertebrae lie deep within the muscles of the back.

The vertebrae are held together by ligaments to form a firm but flexible support structure, the spinal column. The bones of the spine are jointed; in the horse, there are approximately 200 joints in the back, neck, and tail. These joints allow the vertebrae and thus the spinal column to move. The joints and their connecting ligaments effectively handle stresses placed on the column by allowing it to bend but not break.

Numerous muscles are attached to the vertebrae, enabling the horse to move the spinal column at the joints between the vertebrae. Even though the movement between any two vertebrae is small, the cumulative movement of the back and neck is extensive. As the horse raises and lowers its head, vertebrae of the neck and back undergo considerable movement. Horses require movement of the spinal column for proper execution of gaits and for agility in athletic endeavors.

Within each vertebra lies a portion of the nervous system, the spinal cord. The spinal cord passes through the center of each vertebra as it travels from the brain down through the spinal column. As the cord descends, nerves branch off and exit at holes, or foramens, between vertebrae. These branching nerves carry information from the brain to all the organs, muscles, tissues, and cells of the body. This information may instruct a muscle to contract or relax, a gland to secrete, or a tissue to repair damage. The nerves also carry information from the body to the brain. A vast amount of information—about the extent of tissue damage, the location of pain, heat, or cold, or the position of the body and its extremities—is transmitted back to the brain. Since the nervous system integrates and controls the functions of all the tissues and cells, there must be undisturbed nerve transmission in both directions for the body to function properly.

FUNCTIONS OF THE SPINAL COLUMN

The spinal column provides many crucial functions for the body. The most obvious is support. The natural rigidity of the spine enables the horse to carry weight over the thoracic and lumbar vertebrae. The spinal column supplies firm attachment and support for the limbs and the internal organs. It supports the heavy head of the horse while giving shape to the neck and back.

The spinal column also provides a location for attachment for many of the major muscles used in movement. These muscles are used to move the body forward over the limbs in locomotion. Muscles also provide stability to the spinal column by increasing its rigidity. Since the spinal column is a jointed structure, these muscles also create movements such as lateral bend in the back and neck.

The spinal column further serves to protect the central nervous system, or spinal cord. The vertebrae surround the spinal cord, and in order for nerves to reach the tissues of the body, they must exit the spinal column between vertebrae. Nerves are extremely sensitive structures. Research has shown that merely the weight of a dime can cause enough pressure to disrupt function and interfere with communication between the central nervous system and the body tissues. Nerve pressure often occurs at areas where nerves exit between the bones of the spinal column.

Finally, the spinal column offers protection for many internal organs. The kidneys are tucked under the upper lumbar region. The heart and lungs are protected by the thoracic vertebrae and the rib cage. Large blood vessels in the chest and abdomen lie near the spinal column for protection.

. WHAT IS A CHIROPRACTIC . SUBLUXATION?

Chiropractors use the term *subluxation* to describe a specific problem or disease state of the spinal column. A subluxation can be defined as a misaligned vertebra that is "stuck" or unable to move correctly and causing pressure on nerves. Subluxations, therefore, interfere with flexibility of the back and neck and disrupt the functioning of the nervous system.

When movement between two vertebrae is restricted, the horse does not have total flexibility of the spine. Stiffness and resistance to movement results in lowered performance. A horse with stiffness in the midback lacks lateral bending. This becomes apparent in the Quarter Horse that has trouble turning sharply when racing around barrels or performing a reining pattern. A horse with fixations in the low back may lack ability to jump correctly because the back cannot be extended. Rigid joints between cervical vertebrae prevent the horse from coming onto the bit and prevent flexing correctly at the poll.

A restriction between only two vertebrae may not cause significant problems in performance. Restrictions, however, will accumulate. As the spine gradually loses flexibility, the horse compensates by shifting weight or moving a limb differently. As the number of restrictions and compensations accumulate, the horse changes its way of going and becomes "off." At this point, there is often no lameness present. What the horseman notices is unusual, perhaps indefinable, gait abnormalities that vary from limb to limb and change depending on gait and the movement being performed.

One common problem encountered in equine chiropractic care is fixation or subluxations of the sacroiliac joints. These joints connect the iliac bones of the pelvis to the vertebral column at the sacrum. The normal movement at these joints is limited but necessary for proper movement of the rear limb. Subluxations of the sacroiliac joints result in a series of gait problems that develop over time. At first, the sacroiliac fixation shortens the stride of that rear limb. For example, a subluxated right sacroiliac joint may cause a decreased stride of the right rear leg. Often this sacroiliac fixation is accompanied by pelvic rotation. In movement the horse compensates for the pelvic rotation by placing the opposite rear limb inside of the normal line of progression or by rotating the limb as the body weight passes over it. A right sacroiliac fixation can also cause the left rear leg to be placed inside the normal line of progression or the left hock to rotate or wobble. This causes abnormal stress in the joints of that leg. The horse may then shift forward onto the forehand in an attempt to compensate for the lack of flexibility in the sacroiliac joint. Shifting forward will change the center of gravity of the horse's weight, increasing the concussive stresses on the forelimbs. This becomes most serious on the diagonal forelimb and may eventually result in lameness. In addition, the horse compensates for pelvic rotation and fixed sacroiliac joints by transferring stress to the lower back, causing further complications in the lumbar vertebrae. Horses with sacroiliac fixations may display some or all of these compensations. The sooner the sacroiliac subluxation is corrected, the fewer compensations will develop.

A vertebral subluxation can also cause problems in the nervous system. This generally occurs at areas where the spinal nerves exit between two vertebrae. Misalignments between vertebrae cause pressure to be exerted on these sensitive nerves. This pressure may cause local pain in the back or neck. Nerve pressure may also create pain that radiates the entire length of a limb; an example is sciatic neuralgia, which causes nerve pain down the entire length of a rear limb, resulting in gait changes or lameness. The cause of this type of lameness often will go undiagnosed because it is in the spinal column and not in the joints of the limb.

Nerve pressure alters the flow of information that is necessary for proper integration of the functions of the body. Every movement, from simple swishing of the tail to the piaffe in dressage, requires a constant synchronization of muscles in contraction and relaxation. If proper nerve messages to muscles are obstructed, this coordination will falter. Minor interferences may result in only slight changes in performance. In high levels of competition, however, these slight changes may result in an unsuccessful performance. Lack of muscle coordination can cause missteps resulting in damage to the joints and tendons of the legs.

Disruptions of nerve transmissions are capable of affecting many other tissues of the body. Subluxations have been incriminated in decreased or asymmetrical sweating patterns, changes in estrus cycles, and chronic abdominal pain.

Chiropractic care also provides techniques for the adjustment of other joints of the body beside those of the spinal column. The knee, shoulder, and jaw are examples of joints that can be adjusted. The purpose of the extremity techniques is to restore the mobility and integrity of joints.

WHAT CAUSES SUBLUXATIONS?

Traumatic and stressful situations present themselves daily to the performance horse. Saddles, riders, confinement, and sustained vigorous exercise can all cause problems in the spinal column. Injury or trauma to the spinal column is the most common cause of vertebral subluxations. Injuries may be major, such as those sustained in trailer accidents, serious falls, or being cast in a stall. Minor traumas occur almost daily in slips, stumbles, and missteps. Simple movements such as jerking on the lead shank may cause a back or neck problem. Athletic competition predisposes the horse to minor traumas in joints, ligaments, and muscles. Minor traumas tend to accumulate in the spinal column. Symptoms will then develop over time.

Conformation faults predispose the horse to back problems. Horses with long backs have additional strain on the ligaments and muscles that support the back. Lack of angulation in limbs increases the jarring forces acting on the spinal column. A horse simply may not be suited to a desired activity because of its conformation.

Performance horses spend considerable amounts of time being transported between stables and shows, and this is often a source of trauma. A trailer with poor suspension will cause muscle fatigue in the horse that predisposes it to injury. The horse may not always be able to brace for sudden stops or turns. When horses are left to ride loose in a stock trailer, they most often prefer to ride facing the rear. Slant-load trailers give the horse additional stability.

Trauma to the spinal column can occur during birth. A difficult delivery that requires forcible extraction may cause initial misalignments in the soft, formative spine of the newborn foal. These misalignments may set up a pattern of spinal problems that may affect the horse in its performance years.

Constant confinement decreases balance and coordination. The confined horse is not free to buck and roll in a natural attempt to loosen its back. The horse does not learn how to work over uneven ground and lacks coordination of foot movements. Grazing is a natural movement that increases the muscular conditioning of the back and neck while also stretching the neck and lifting the back. The horse should have a minimum period of turn-out each day as well as the largest box stall possible.

Horses are used in a wide variety of activities such as jumping, racing, and dressage. The daily consequences of these athletic performances are minute traumas to joints, ligaments, tendons, bones, and muscles. Each equine sport has different effects on the spinal column due to the requirements of the activity. Dressage, for example, depends on freedom of spinal movement to achieve lengthening of the top line and engagement of hindquarters. Jumping horses need efficient flexion and extension of the back. The racing Thoroughbred requires efficient spinal movement to achieve stride length and speed.

Problems in the back of the horse often are traced to lack of ability in the rider. The balance and coordination of the horse changes when loads are placed on its back. If the rider is unbalanced, the horse has to compensate. When the rider drops the head to look at his hands, approximately ten pounds is added to the weight on the forehand. Failure of the horse to compensate effectively for unbalanced loads may cause subluxations.

Improper, poorly fitting tack can also cause problems in the spinal column. A common fault is an ill-fitting or improperly positioned saddle. A saddle should fit the horse without the use of expensive pads. A narrow tree or a saddle placed too far forward interferes with movement of the horse's shoulders. This interference may cause the horse to tighten the muscles over the withers, with resulting subluxations of the upper thoracic vertebrae. The improper use of side reins, draw reins, leg stretchers, head checks, and hobbles can contribute to back and neck problems.

As horses age, the spine accumulates the effects of all the large and small injuries, traumas, and misuses that have occurred. Any one injury may not be very significant, but accumulation over years eventually will decrease performance ability. Chiropractic care is often an effective therapy for the older horse that is not performing up to its potential.

Lack of proper care in trimming and shoeing the feet can result in many compensations in the spinal column. Long toes, high heels, small shoes, and uneven hoof walls interfere with movement and posture. Horses must be centered properly over the shoes and the structures of the foot for proper movement.

Stressful conditions in the horse's environment can also cause subluxations. Lack of companionship (human or horse), a change of barns, and loss of a stablemate are some of the causes that increase tension and stress.

WHAT ARE THE SYMPTOMS OF A SUBLUXATION?

Subluxations of the spinal column produce many symptoms in the horse. The most common effect of a subluxation is pain. Horses in pain will compensate in gait or posture and often resist or refuse to perform. The following is a list of symptoms that may indicate pain from a subluxation.

- Abnormal posture: standing in a tucked-up or spread-out posture; placing one limb abnormally.

- Discomfort when saddling: actively resisting the saddle or the cinch.

- Discomfort when riding: slow to warm up or "cold-backed"; dipping the back when mounted, bucking, difficulty with sitting trot.

- Evasions: extending head and neck and hollowing back.

- Wringing tail.

- Pinning ears.

- Grinding teeth.

- Refusal or unwillingness over jumps.

- Refusal or resistance in performing lateral or collected movements.

- Development of unusual behavior patterns: sudden refusals or resistance.

- Facial expression of apprehension or pain.

- Sensitivity to touch: uncomfortable to a brush or light palpation.

- Bad attitude: biting, unfriendliness.

Subluxations may cause changes in muscle coordination and flexibility that affect the performance ability of the horse. These symptoms may be:

- Unusual, perhaps indefinable, gait abnormalities that vary from limb to limb and change depending on gait; the rider or trainer may be aware that the horse is "off" but is unable to pinpoint the problem; the horses is not lame, but also not performing up to potential.

- Lack of coordination in gaits.

- Stiffness when coming out of stall.

- Stiffness in lateral movements of neck or back.

- Muscle atrophy: loss of muscle mass over the pelvis or in portions of an upper limb.

- Rope-walking or plaiting: placing one or both rear limbs too far inside normal progression of foot during movement.

- Shortened stride in one or two limbs.

- Inability to engage rear quarters or flex the lumbosacral region.

- Inability to lengthen topline.

- Improper frame.

- Decreased stride length.

- Difficulty flexing at the poll.

- Not coming onto the bit.

- Tilting head to the side.

- Obscure lameness.

- On one line or resisting one rein.

- Rider cannot sit centered on horse.

- Dragging toes or unusual shoe wear.

- Difficulty in particular gait such as rack or canter.

Subluxations also cause symptoms by interfering with the nerve supply to other tissues such as the skin, glands, and blood vessels. Some of the symptoms that result may be unusual body- or tail-rubbing, increased sensitivity to heat or cold, and asymmetrical sweating or lack of sweating.

These lists of symptoms caused by subluxations are not meant to be complete, but they illustrate the variety of problems that are possible with subluxations of the spinal column.

EXAMINING THE HORSE
FOR SUBLUXATIONS

Chiropractors are specially trained to locate and correct subluxations. An equine chiropractor will examine the horse's gait, posture, muscle balance and tone, vertebral position, and joint mobility and will correlate that information with facts about the horse's symptoms and medical history. Trainers, riders, and owners should also learn to examine the spinal column for problems. Examining the spinal column during a prepurchase checkup is just as important as examining any other area of the horse. The following sections describe several simple procedures to evaluate the spinal column of the horse.

CASE HISTORY

Mentally review the past and present performance record. What are the current problems of the horse? Is the horse working below previous levels of performance? Where is the resistance to movement? Is the horse stiffer when moving to one side? Is there a change in the horse's attitude toward work and toward its handlers? What medications need to be administered frequently and why? Are there subtle shifts or difficulties in gaits without apparent lameness? These performance problems are often the first indications that the spinal column is not functioning properly. The perceptive horseman is often aware that "something" is wrong but may be unable to pinpoint the problem. In many cases the horse is thought to be lazy, misbehaving, or unresponsive to training. The horse may be willing but restricted by stiffness or pain.

POSTURE

Examine the horse as it stands on a firm level surface. Allow the horse to assume a natural position at the end of the lead shank. After observing its posture, move the horse several steps and note similarities or differences in the previous stance. Look for constant resting of one foot, abnormal foot placement, tucked-up posture, or a stretched-out stance. Observe the topline of the horse. Are there prominent bumps, or one broad area in the back that seems elevated? Is there a tendency toward a weak or sway back? Sore, stiff backs may cause the horse to adopt certain postures that minimize pain, such as standing tucked-up.

Note the horse's head placement. Is the head tilted, placed abnormally high or low? Is the neck inverted or held rigidly? These symptoms may indicate problems in the cervical portion of the spine.

GAIT AND PERFORMANCE

The sensitive and aware rider senses gait problems while in the saddle. The rider may become aware of resistance, stiffness, lack of impulsion, or discomfort in the horse. Riders can feel tension, apprehension, or lack of rhythm. It is often beneficial, however, for the rider to watch the horse move with someone else up. Does the horse move one leg in a short stride? Does the horse look properly collected?

An analysis of gait should be done while the horse walks straight away from the examiner and while circling on a lunge line. This is best done as another person handles the horse, so that the examiner can concentrate on movement. Observation of gait is difficult. It takes practice to train the eyes to record all the movements of the limbs, back, and head that are occurring at once. Two methods may help make gait analysis easier.

1. Focus on one area at a time, such as one joint or one leg.

2. Slightly blur your vision to observe the entire picture the horse creates as it moves.

When the horse is walking on a straight line away from you, watch only the top of the horse's buttocks or hips at first. Does one side drop and one side stay high and fixed? There should be equal rise and fall of both hips. If one side of the pelvis seems to drop excessively, this often indicates that the opposite side has a fixed or locked sacroiliac joint. Now have the horse trotted away on a straight line and again observe the hip movement. The rise and fall of the hips should be equal at the trot also.

Walk the horse straight away again and this time observe the hocks as the horse moves its weight over this joint. Does one hock seem unstable or "wobbly"? Does one hock twist to the outside as it bears weight? This may indicate that the pelvis has rotated, causing one leg to be functionally longer than the other. As the horse moves weight over that long limb, the hock will twist slightly or the foot will be placed inside of the normal progression to compensate.

Observe the horse on a lunge line. Does the horse resist in one direction more than the other? This may indicate stiffness in the back as the horse attempts to bend into the circle. Look for stumbling, short strides, rope-walking, lack of back movement, abnormal hip movement, and abnormal joint motion.

MUSCLE PALPATION

Horses in athletic condition should display muscles of good tone that are symmetrical from side to side. Move the mane and tail to compare the symmetry of the neck and the buttocks. Pay attention to the muscles over the scapulas, or shoulder blades. The muscles should be firm without being too hard or too soft. Take the time to develop a feel for good muscle tone. Horses with stiff and painful backs will often have exceptionally tense back muscles. The muscles feel rigid, and the horse will drop to avoid pressure. Normal muscles are not painful to palpation of moderate pressure. If the horse moves away from a light touch, ripples the skin excessively, or behaves defensively, the muscles may be sore. Sore muscles can arise from training and injury, but may also signal the presence of subluxations.

Horses in good condition do not necessarily have excessive definition to their muscles. Muscle definition is the appearance of prominent depressions or lines between muscle groups. Excessive muscle definition is often a symptom of muscles under tension. Muscular tension prevents freedom of movement, causing difficulty in work and performance.

SPINAL PALPATION

Palpate down the center of the back or along the spinal column in the thoracic lumbar regions for prominent elevations or bumps. The tops of the vertebrae should feel level. A prominent vertebra may indicate that the bone has moved out of position. Older performance horses often have a prominent area—sometimes called a "hunter's bump"—in the spine just ahead of the pelvic region. If the horse also seems stiff in the lower back and has difficulty engaging or putting the rear limbs under the body, these prominent vertebrae may signal the need for chiropractic adjustments.

Compare the two prominences at the top of the hips near the midline. These bony areas are the uppermost portion of the horse's pelvis. They should be level. If one side is higher than the other, this may indicate that the pelvis has rotated.

Palpate down the vertebrae at the sides of the neck. For the location of the cervical vertebrae, turn to the diagram at the beginning of this chapter. You will see that they are located in the lower one-third of the neck. As you palpate, note any vertebrae that seem to be more prominent on one side of the neck. Prominent vertebrae may indicate a lateral deviation or subluxation.

SPINAL MOBILITY

A horseman can determine if problems exist in the spinal column of the horse by assessing the joint mobility of the column. A horse should be able to move the column freely in all ranges of motion with no tension under saddle, in harness, or from the ground. The horse should be able to bend his neck equally in both directions, touching his nose to his side.

To examine the range of motion in the cervical region, stand by the horse's shoulder and gently pull on the halter until the horse fully flexes the neck to his side. Do not allow the horse to move his legs. Repeat for the other side of the neck. Repeat the examination using a carrot as bait. Resistance or unequal ability indicates cervical stiffness and possibly a subluxation. The rider may already have noticed this lack of flexibility because there is increased resistance on one rein.

The horseman can also assess flexibility in the thoracic and lumbar vertebrae. To determine lateral flexibility or bend, stand parallel to and face the horse at the flank area.

Grasp the base of the tail with one hand and place the palm of the opposite hand on the back, contacting the upper portion of one vertebra. Pulling the base of the tail toward the examiner should cause the back to bend around the other hand. With practice, contact can be made on individual vertebrae and the amount of lateral bend can be assessed in separate spinal segments. Repeat this procedure on the other side of the horse. If one side is stiffer than the other, subluxations may be interfering with spinal flexibility.

A horse should be able to drop or extend the back as well as flex or lift the back. Position yourself above the horse. You can stand on two small bales of hay stacked next to the horse or on a mounting block. Whatever support you choose should be stable, with no sharp edges. Using moderate downward pressure with arms extended, apply pressure to vertebrae in several locations. The back should dip slightly, indicating normal extension. Except for the region close to the withers the back should feel supple, not tight and rigid. To assess the flexion or lift of the back, offer the horse a carrot held between and slightly behind the forelimbs. Watch the back lift as the horse flexes its neck to reach for the carrot. Stiffness or lack of movement may indicate the presence of subluxations of the spine.

▪ HOW ARE SUBLUXATIONS ▪ CORRECTED?

When subluxations in the spine are identified, the veterinary chiropractor will attempt a correction of the misalignment. This correction is called an *adjustment*. An adjustment is a short, rapid thrust onto a vertebra in the direction that will free the vertebra from its fixed position and replace it in a normal position.

Chiropractic adjustments are applied to the specific vertebrae involved in subluxations, as identified by the chiropractic examination. A horse may have one or several misaligned or subluxated vertebrae. An adjustment is made directly on the long process of the vertebra. In horses, the length of the vertebral processes gives the adjuster mechanical advantage. An adjustment also uses a very specific alignment to move through the angles of the joints that link the vertebrae. The veterinary chiropractor requires an intimate knowledge of the anatomy of each vertebra and how these vertebrae are joined. A properly aligned thrust restores joint motion without the need for a lot of force. An improperly aligned thrust will be ineffective if not detrimental to the joints in the back.

The adjustment releases the "stuck" vertebra and re stores spinal alignment, thus eliminating nerve pressure and interference. The body can then repair tissues and restore function.

Chiropractic is a diverse field and there are many different types of techniques that are used. Most veterinary chiropractors will use only their hands to adjust the vertebrae of horses. Some doctors use a small impacting device, called an activator, to move the vertebra. The device is effective due to its specificity and speed. Some individuals use mallets to strike on pads placed over the vertebrae; this technique can be effective if done properly by a very skilled individual, but it can create more problems if it is done incorrectly. Some "so-called" chiropractors employ methods that rely on pulling or jerking on legs to adjust the spine. These techniques are not specific to the individual affected vertebral joints and are potentially harmful to the joints of the legs. These latter techniques should be avoided in favor of techniques that are specific as well as safe.

Veterinary chiropractors also manipulate the joints of the legs as well as the jaw. Adjusting the extremities is one specialty in chiropractic. One joint that is often misaligned is the knee. The horse's knee, or carpus, consists of two rows of bones. Occasionally, one of the small bones in the upper row slides forward, which causes changes in the mechanical use of the knee. The result may be carpitis (knee inflammation) or even a fracture of this bone. In addition, when a carpal bone slides forward, the nerve running down the back of the knee may be trapped in the soft tissue and produce pain. This condition is similar to carpal tunnel syndrome that affects the wrists of humans. In horses, carpal tunnel syndrome may mimic the pain caused by navicular disease.

The jaw joint, or temporomandibular joint (TMJ), can also become misaligned or fixed. The horse with a TMJ problem may resist the bit, need dental work frequently, or grind his teeth. There are special techniques used in chiropractic to adjust the joints of the jaw.

The most common misunderstanding concerning chiropractic care is why several adjustments may be needed. The purpose of an adjustment is to realign the spine. The muscles and ligaments of the horse must be able to maintain the correct spinal alignment. When an orthodontist works to straighten teeth, he applies a rigid brace directly to the teeth. Chiropractors cannot do this for the spine. They may need to make several adjustments before the body accepts and maintains the correct alignment. Most horses will show significant improvement in one to four adjustments. Chronic spinal problems may take longer to respond fully. Horses that are basically sound, with a conformation suited to the desired activity, will respond quickly to adjustments and maintain spinal alignments longer.

• SPINAL HEALTH CARE •

Since proper functioning of the back and neck is vital to performance, care of the back should be a major concern for horsemen. Here we will consider the proper management of the horse to ensure correct functioning of the spinal column, and the specific techniques that can be used to maintain this function.

The conformation of the horse should be considered when selecting a horse for a particular use. Horse breeds have been modified selectively to function best in a variety of performance types. Selecting an individual solely on the basis of breed or halter conformation is no guarantee, however, that the animal will function successfully as an athlete. Study those horses that are winning consistently. Bear in mind that long-backed horses are more prone to muscle and ligament injuries, while those with straight shoulders are predisposed to front-leg problems.

Massage and muscle therapy is beneficial in the continued spinal health of a horse. Massage increases blood supply, which brings nutrition to muscles and carries away waste materials. Massage relaxes tight, tense muscles that interfere with performance. Massage also helps in the healing of tissues by removing adhesions and speeding removal of fluid. Massage enhances the horse's response to chiropractic adjustment and helps the spine maintain the correction. (See Chapter Four on massage.)

Horses are more prone to subluxations and spinal trauma when soft tissues such as ligaments, tendons, and muscles are not conditioned for work. Interval training, adequate warm-up periods, and varying the type of activity will help with conditioning the equine athlete. Training that depends on the proper function of the back, as in dressage, should proceed gradually so that the back is not damaged.

Make sure that the saddle fits the horse. The most frequent problems encountered are saddles that are too small for the horse or are placed too far forward. A small saddle centers the rider's weight in one area; a larger saddle distributes weight over a larger area. If the tree is too narrow, pressure is placed on the thoracic vertebrae. Saddles placed too far forward often interfere with the movement of the scapulas (shoulder blades). The panels of the saddle should touch the back along their entire length. Check the saddle for uneven wear, for asymmetry in the tree or panels, and for a broken tree.

Saddle pads should dissipate pressure points from the saddle, thus a properly fitting saddle will not require special pads. Excellent pads are made from wool fleece, since the natural crimp in the fibers absorbs pressure. Wool felt lacks the absorptive property because the fibers have been compressed. "Orthopedic" pads of closed-cell foam also serve the purpose of eliminating pressure points.

Avoid forcing the horse in training with devices that aggravate spinal restrictions. Tying the head to a stirrup to increase flexibility may only aggravate the cervical subluxations that caused the restriction in the first place. Side reins may help teach the horse to use the neck properly, but they also may cause subluxations when the horse is forced into a frame too soon. Constant jerking on the lead shank as a correction in the young horse causes tension in the muscles of the neck. The horse learns to keep the head elevated, putting an abnormal curve in the neck and creating a predisposition for problems in this area.

It is virtually impossible to maintain spinal alignment when the horse's feet do not have proper care. A horse with one short or one long leg can be brought into balance at the feet with variations in hoof wall and pad height. This will help maintain spinal alignment. Employ the most expert farrier you can find, one with knowledge of what is expected of the horse in performance.

Most performance horses are confined to box stalls with limited amounts of free or turn-out time. The more time a horse spends in a stall the less coordination he will have.

This limits balance and increases the chance of trauma to joints in the back and extremities. Bucking and rolling are the horse's natural ways of adjusting its own spine. Make sure that the horse has enough free movement to get the "kinks" out.

An effective adjunct in the care of the equine back is acupuncture and acupressure. (See Chapter One on acupuncture.) Some of the more basic techniques can be learned by horsemen, but the full range of techniques in either method should be attempted only by veterinarians with advanced training. The combination of acupuncture and chiropractic often results in faster and longer-acting responses to spinal adjustments.

▪ CHIROPRACTIC TECHNIQUES ▪ FOR HORSEMEN

There are many techniques that the interested and involved horseman can learn to increase the function of the back of the horse. Spinal flexibility is important and there are several ways to increase mobility with simple exercises. Increasing flexibility in the neck is produced by repetitions of range-of-motion exercises. Stand at the horse's shoulder, hold the halter, and gently pull the horse's head to the side. Encourage the horse to flex as far as possible. Carrots can be used as bait, but the best method is to teach the horse to respond to your instructions. The horse should be able to touch his nose to his body just behind the shoulder area. If the neck seems stiff, encourage more movement with gentle pressure, but never with force. Always perform all equine exercises with the horse's ability in mind. Allow the neck to straighten and repeat the procedure several times. Exercise both sides but concentrate on the side that is the stiffer.

The horse owner can increase the flexibility of the back

by gently moving the thoracic and lumbar regions through normal ranges of motion. Place two bales of hay alongside the horse just as you would if you were using these bales to mount the horse. Mounting blocks and crates are usually not tall enough for this procedure. Ladders and other such objects are rarely stable enough and may be dangerous if a horse steps through an open rung. When you are high enough to be over the back of the horse, place the heel of your hand on the midline of the back. Start just ahead of the pelvis. Apply steady downward pressure until the back dips slightly. Move your hands forward onto the next vertebra and again apply pressure. Move gradually up the spine, applying pressure to each vertebra. Do not apply a lot of force and do not "hit" the area or drop down suddenly. Repeating the procedure will gently move the joints of the back into extension. If the joints remain rigid at one or more areas, a chiropractic adjustment may be needed before this exercise is effective.

The ability of the horse to bend laterally can also be improved with exercises. The method for this exercise is similar to the method described previously in evaluating lateral bend. Stand at the side of the horse near the flank. Grasp the top of the tail with one hand and place the heel of the other hand on the tops of the vertebrae. Start just above the pelvis. Bend the horse around the hand resting on the vertebra. Encourage the horse to work to increase flexibility. Proceed gradually up the spine. Never force the horse with this procedure or apply sudden forceful movements. Again, resistance and lack of bend may indicate that a chiropractic adjustment is needed before normal function can be restored.

The entire spinal column of the horse can be stretched by having the horse dip his head between his front legs to take a carrot from your hand. You may need to teach the horse this exercise by gradually moving the carrot into the correct position. Never force a horse to do this exercise by pulling on the halter.

The horse can learn to exercise the abdominal muscles in order to increase the lift or rounding of the back. Encourage the horse to elevate the topline by applying finger pressure to the abdomen. Watch the back. The topline should rise. Have the horse hold this position for a few moments by keeping pressure on the abdomen. Allow the muscles to relax and then repeat the procedure several times. This horse "sit-up" effectively works the abdominal muscles.

Simple exercises can increase the range of motion in several joints of the extremities. The joints to be exercised should be free of major pathologies such as bone chips or arthritis. If your veterinarian has been treating the joint, ask for his or her advice before working on that joint. Never force joints with these exercises. Discontinue any joint mobilization if the horse seriously objects or is lame afterward. Always be aware of your personal safety when working with the legs of horses.

The scapula, or shoulder blade, of the horse is not connected to the rib cage by joints, but is attached by muscles and ligaments. One exercise to improve the movement of the scapula is a leg lift. Lift the forelimb by grasping the cannon bone in one hand and the pastern with the other, keeping all the joints of the leg flexed. Elevate the entire limb toward the back and watch as the scapula rises and becomes almost level with the top of the withers. Notice any resistance or stiffness with this exercise. Allow the limb to relax or drop and repeat the procedure two to four times. Repeat for the other side. When you perform this exercise, make sure that you keep your back as straight as possible and lift with power from your legs.

Another exercise will loosen the scapula as well as the shoulder joint. While holding one of the forelimbs, move forward so as to stand in front of the horse. Pull or stretch the limb forward. This exercise pulls the scapula down the rib cage while also extending the shoulder joint.

The knees of the horse can be tractioned to increase

mobility. Lift the horse's leg with one hand and place your opposite forearm tightly behind the knee. With gentle and steady pressure, flex the horse's knee around your arm. Repeat for the other knee. Occasionally you may hear noises, or "pops," with this exercise; this is normal.

The pastern joints can be mobilized by grasping the hoof in both hands. Rotate the foot at the pastern joint in both directions. Do not place abnormal stress on the fetlock point, since it does not rotate.

The temporomandibular (jaw) joints may be involved when a horse resists the bit, needs frequent floating (filing), or grinds his teeth. A simple exercise for the joints of the jaw is traction and compression. For the first part of this technique, stand alongside the horse's neck facing the same direction as the horse. Hold each side of the lower jaw or mandible with your hands. Apply steady pressure upward toward the horse's ears. As the horse relaxes into your hands, the jaw can be rocked gently from side to side. This portion of the exercise compresses the joint. Next, move your fingers down the side of the mandible until they slide into a slight depression. Hook your fingers in this depression and pull downward with a gentle and steady pressure. As the horse relaxes, gently rock the mandible from side to side. This maneuver applies traction to both jaw joints. One series of compression and traction is generally sufficient to increase mobility. If the jaw joints seems very stiff, a chiropractic adjustment may be required.

• VETERINARY CHIROPRACTIC CARE •

Chiropractic care can be a cost-effective way to maintain the performance ability of the horse. Chiropractic works to eliminate the source of the pain or problem, and to increase the overall function of the spinal column. If you

believe that your horse may benefit from the services of an animal chiropractor, how do you choose a practitioner?

Always have your veterinarian examine the horse first to determine if problems exist that require medical or surgical attention.

The American Veterinary Chiropractic Association trains and certifies chiropractors and veterinarians in the art and science of animal adjusting. Chiropractors with this advanced training are able to accept animal cases by the referral of a veterinarian. Ask your veterinarian to make this referral for you. Veterinarians with certification in animal chiropractic may be called to see your horse without a referral.

If no certified animal chiropractor is available in your area, perhaps your veterinarian will work with a chiropractor to provide your horse with spinal care. The chiropractor's knowledge of the spine and adjusting ability in combination with the veterinarian's knowledge of horses often creates a very successful team approach.

When selecting a chiropractor for your horse, be wary of exaggerated claims. Performance horses often have many problems and many compensations. Chiropractic care, just like traditional veterinary medical and surgical therapy, cannot solve all the problems of horses. Some equine problems are permanent and some diseases are progressive despite the best health care.

Have realistic expectations. Do not expect the veterinary chiropractor to be able to solve long-standing or multiple problems with one adjustment. Healing takes time.

Chiropractic promises to be an important portion of equine health care. Spinal adjustments can increase flexibility of the equine athlete and provide a nonmedical way of eliminating pain. Obscure and recurring lameness is common in the equine industry and chiropractic care may provide the answer for some of these cases. Finally, when used as a preventative health-care approach, chiropractic offers tremendous value in the maintenance of the performance horse.

More information on animal chiropractic and certified animal chiropractors is available from the American Veterinary Chiropractic Association, P.O. Box 249, Port Byron, IL 61275; (309) 523-3995.

HOMEOPATHY

DEVA KAUR KHALSA, V.M.D.

INTRODUCTION

Homeopathic remedies have been used to treat illness in people and animals since the late eighteenth century. Homeopathic treatment stimulates the organism to cure itself. Within each individual, there are natural mechanisms that work to correct imbalances and maintain a healthy equilibrium. Homeopathic treatment works with the body's natural forces to promote health. These remedies must be carefully selected, taking into consideration both the problem to be treated and the particular and individual way the illness presents itself in the animal.

The substances that are used to formulate homeopathic remedies are wide and varied. Many herbs and minerals are used. Insects, poisons, and modern medicinals such as antibiotics also are used in the preparation of homeopathic remedies. Quite frankly, a homeopathic remedy can be made from just about anything. Each remedy has specific and particular modes of action and is used when indicated in an illness or injury.

Homeopathic preparations are called "remedies" and the definition of a homeopathic remedy lies not in what it is made from but in how it is prepared. The word *potency* is used to indicate the strength of the remedy. The remedies are diluted sequentially. The substance is diluted with 1 drop of original tincture and 9 drops of alcohol to make an "x" potency, or with 1 drop to 99 drops of alcohol to make a "c" potency. After each dilution, the bottle is shaken vigorously. The potency depends on the number of sequential dilutions. For example, a 30x potency has been diluted 1 to 9, thirty times. A 1m potency has been diluted 1,000 times, a 10m potency has been diluted 10,000 times. Consequently, a homeopathic remedy has little physical or molecular substance remaining. A fact that many beginners find difficult to assimilate is that as the remedy becomes more dilute, it becomes more powerful. Thus a 30x potency is considered more powerful than a 6x potency. The shaking (succussion) and grinding (trituration) are of absolute importance, since it is here that the subtle energies of the remedy are released. Interestingly, because these remedies contain infinitesimal amounts of substance they cannot be traced in any of the body's tissues or fluids, including the urine, blood, and saliva. These remedies cannot produce the toxic side effects of the original substance.

Homeopathic preparations often are placed on small lactose pellets for oral administration. Remedies may also be administered in a water-based solution. Horses readily eat the milk-sugar (lactose) tablets, and a dose would consist of several of these tablets or a dropperful of the water-based solution given by mouth. It is not necessary to count out the tablets individually, since the amount of the tablets given is not as important as the frequency of the dosage. It is important to remember that homeopathic remedies are very sensitive to radiation and strong odors. Keep them at least fifteen feet from microwave ovens when you store them. Also keep them away from computers, televisions, microwave towers, and any other devices that emit strong radiation. Do not open or use the remedies in the presence of strong odors such as camphor, mothballs, Tiger Balm, mint, coffee, or turpentine. Both electromagnetic forces and strong odors could inactivate the remedy. In addition, do not leave the remedies in extreme heat or strong sunlight for protracted periods of time.

Homeopathic remedies can be ordered by anyone, up to a 1m potency, from homeopathic pharmacies that exist throughout the world. It is recommended that you keep a stock of homeopathic remedies in a kit at home so they will be readily available when needed. A list of some of the pharmacies that exist in the United States is presented in an appendix at the end of this chapter.

Homeopathy is a therapeutic method that applies clinically the Law of Similars and uses medicinal substances at small or infinitesimal doses. During his time, Hippocrates said, "The same agents which provide the disease cure it." It was not until the end of the eighteenth century that a German doctor, Christian-Samuel Hahnemann, studied this concept and formulated the Law of Similars. I will give two examples of this law. Allium cepa is a remedy made from the common onion. It might be chosen as the indicated remedy for a patient with a common cold and watery discharge from the nose and eyes. These are the same symptoms that appear when a healthy individual cuts an onion. Belladonna, if taken in its crude form, will rapidly produce a high fever, dilated pupils, and a throbbing pulse. This remedy would be used as a homeopathic preparation to treat someone with influenza who has similar symptoms.

Homeopathic therapeutics acts in the same sense as the normal reactions of the organism. It works together with the healing forces in the animal, and stimulates these forces to be more efficient. Two people can experience the same cold differently. One may want to be left alone in a dark room and another may want constant attention. One may be thirsty while the other is thirstless. The appropriate remedy is chosen by the symptoms the patient presents. Thus, the homeopathic method produces an individualization of treatment. The physical, mental, and emotional makeup of the individual is considered.

Modalities are the differences and modifications of symptoms. For example: Is the condition relieved by warmth or cold? Is the animal better after moving or after resting? What time of day is the problem worse? Is a fever accompanied by great thirst or no thirst? You will notice these modalities in the descriptions of the remedies below. They are extremely valuable in choosing the correct remedy.

• HOMEOPATHIC FIRST AID •

Arnica   *Arnica montana.* Prepared from the whole fleshy plant.

Arnica is used primarily for wounds and injuries. It should be used in every case of trauma and muscular strain. Arnica can be used to prevent stiffness after a horse has been worked hard. This remedy should also be used before and after surgery. Given after parturition it will hasten the recovery of bruised tissues, and if it is used during pregnancy, it will encourage an easier labor. Arnica may also be used topically as a tincture or salve for bruised tendons, ligaments, or muscles.

POTENCY AND DOSAGE: Arnica can be used in any potency. The 30x potency is good to use in any situation.

Trauma and muscular strain A 30x potency once an hour for four doses, then follow with one dose three or four times a day.

To prevent stiffness One or two doses before exercising, and a few doses following exercise.

For surgery Three times a day for a few days before surgery, then six times a day after surgery.

Pregnancy One dose a few times a week during pregnancy, several doses during parturition, then three times a day for a week after parturition.

TOPICALLY: Apply as a moist wrap, using Arnica tincture diluted 1:10, or apply as a cream or ointment on the affected area. Do not use topically on *open* wounds or cuts. Arnica should be used *orally* for open wounds or cuts, bruises, and sprains, and *topically only* for closed bruises and sprains.

Calendula *Calendula officinalis,* marigold. The tincture is prepared from the leaves and the flowers.

Calendula is the remedy to be considered when dealing with open wounds, such as cuts, abrasions, and lacerations. It is used primarily as a topical agent. The tincture can be diluted from 1:5 to 1:10 and the area should be flushed liberally or a moist pack can be wrapped around the area. As the open wound begins to heal, Calendula can be applied a few times daily in the form of an ointment or salve. This remedy, when applied topically to an open wound, works rapidly to stop bleeding, promote healing, and prevent local infection. Calendula also helps to prevent the formation of scar tissue. I once treated a gray Arabian mare that had become tangled in a barbed wire fence and had incurred severe lacerations all over her hind legs. One laceration above the vaginal area was more than 3 inches deep. She was given Arnica 30x orally several times a day and all the wounds were flushed or wrapped with diluted Calendula tincture three to four times a day. The mare healed uneventfully, very swiftly, and with no swelling of the affected tissues and minimal scarring.

Hypericum   *Hypericum   perforatum,*   St.-John's-wort.
Prepared from the fresh whole plant.

Hypericum is the great remedy for injuries to nerves,
particularly where the termination of nerves is involved.
It can also produce excellent results when used for spinal
injuries, especially in cases where the lower back (coccygeal area) is involved. It is an important remedy for any
puncture wound and can, in that instance, be used in conjunction with the remedy Ledum. These two remedies
should always be used in any injury likely to lead to
tetanus.

Hypericum is to damage of the nervous system as Arnica is to muscular damage. Hypericum is an excellent
first-aid remedy; it can be used as a homeopathic potency
orally and as a topical wash or ointment.

Hypericum rapidly alleviates pain from injuries to
nerves in the extremities. Anyone who has ever taken Hypericum after crushing a finger or toe can happily attest
to this.

POTENCY AND DOSAGE: Hypericum can always be
used in the 30x potency. Potencies from 6x to 1m can also
be used if indicated. If the thirtieth potency does not appear to alleviate the discomfort, then higher potencies such
as a 1m potency can be used orally. The frequency of the
dosage can range from every half-hour for a few hours after
the injury to three or four times a day.

The tincture of Hypericum can also be diluted 1:10
and flushed into the laceration or puncture wound until
full healing occurs. Calendula and Hypericum tincture can
be combined, diluted, and flushed into the wound. Hypericum ointment and combined Calendula and Hypericum ointment also are available from health food stores
and homeopathic pharmacies.

Ledum   *Ledum palustre,* marsh tea. Prepared from the whole fresh plant.

Ledum is another useful remedy for painful puncture wounds. It is indicated in injuries that manifest a black-and-blue discoloration. Ledum is also a useful remedy for corneal ulcers. It can be used in conjunction with Hypericum for corneal ulcers due to a puncture wound. This remedy is particularly appropriate for puncture wounds that do not bleed. Insect bites can benefit from the use of this remedy. The remedies Hypericum and Apis can also be used with insect bites. Ledum can be used for blunt trauma to the eye in conjunction with Symphytum. Given along with Hypericum, it helps to prevent tetanus. Ledum can be given orally in homeopathic potency.

POTENCY AND DOSAGE: Ledum can be used successfully in the 30x potency, giving one dose several times a day.

Apis   Honeybee venom. Prepared from the whole bee *(Apis mellifica).*

Apis is an important remedy to consider in cases where edema and swelling occur. It is the first remedy to consider after a bee sting. Apis can be used after an insect bite that causes swelling of the tissues. Synovial swellings of joints will benefit. Acute navicular disease, bog spavin, and other joint diseases that incur swelling may show improvement with the use of this remedy. Apis is indicated in cases of edema in the lungs and ascites (fluid) in the abdomen. In kidney problems where there is an abnormally low level of urine being passed, it has been known to promote urination. Two modalities that indicate the need for the remedy Apis are thirstlessness and edema relieved by cold.

POTENCY AND DOSAGE: Chronic problems such as ascites and fluid in the lungs will benefit from using Apis

30x three to four times a day, decreasing the frequency as the condition improves.

Acute problems, such as a bee sting, will benefit from Apis 1m or 10m used hourly for a few doses, although the 30x potency can be used if it is the only one available.

Aconite   *Aconite napellus,* monkshood. Prepared from the whole plant, root, and flower.

Aconite's primary use is for fevers and illnesses that follow a chill—or exposure to a cold wind—and have sudden onset. This remedy should be used in the early stages of all feverish states. It can be used for joints that suddenly become swollen and hot after a horse is chilled. Aconite is an excellent remedy for shock. It is good to use for the horse that is afraid of new places and people. Before a show or a race, Aconite can be combined with the remedy Gelsemium to alleviate the nervousness that can occur when the animal knows he must perform.

The animal that needs Aconite in the beginning of an illness will often show restlessness and anxiety. The horse may appear irritable and frightened. If a temperature occurred suddenly and is rising rapidly, a few doses of Aconite will often nip the problem in the bud if given early enough.

POTENCY AND DOSAGE: Aconite 30x is a fine potency to use, but the 1m potency will often have a more dramatic effect in the more acute inflammatory stage.

Fevers; hot, swollen joints Aconite 1m every fifteen minutes for one hour, repeat after waiting one hour if necessary.

Shows and performance Aconite 30x and Gelsemium 30x every hour or so for a few hours before the show. Begin when the horse starts to exhibit the first signs of nervousness.

Ruta   *Ruta graveolens,* rue. Prepared from the fresh whole plant.

Ruta is the best remedy to use when there is trauma or strain to tendons, ligaments, cartilage, or the periosteum of bone. The 30x potency, used three times a day, is usually sufficient. Ruta can be combined with Arnica when soft-tissue and tendon damage coexist.

Rhus Tox   *Rhus toxidendron,* poison ivy. Prepared from the fresh leaves before flowering.

Rhus tox is a wonderful remedy for arthritis and stiffness that improves after the horse is worked a little. The most important guiding symptom or modality is that the animal shows improvement after slow motion and is stiffer and more painful after rest. It is also an excellent remedy for poison ivy and skin conditions with the same appearance as poison ivy.

The arthritis is worse with cold and wet conditions and better with warmth. The horse may shift his position frequently to become more comfortable. Rhus tox can also be used for sprains and strains that exhibit the same modalities.

Bryonia   *Bryonia alba,* white bryony. Prepared from the root before flowering takes place.

In contrast to the remedy Rhus tox, a lameness that needs Bryonia is always worse after movement and better after resting. Synovitis and painful joint swelling may generally need this remedy. It is an excellent remedy to use in pneumonia where the animal does not want to move and lies on the affected side. The mucous membranes often are dry and the animal is thirsty for large quantities of water when Bryonia is needed for this condition.

Lameness Bryonia 30x two to three times a day.

Pneumonia Bryonia 30x every two hours or Bryonia 1m once an hour for four doses.

Echinacea   Prepared from the whole fresh plant.

Echinacea is an excellent remedy to improve the functioning state of the immune system and to prevent and treat infection. It can be given in the 6x potency two times a day.

Symphytum   *Symphytum officinale,* comfrey. Prepared from the whole fresh root and plant.

This remedy is particularly useful in cases of trauma to the bones and the periosteum. It rapidly speeds up the healing of fractures and decreases the pain caused by the tearing of the periosteum that occurs in sprains. This remedy is also excellent to use in cases of blunt trauma to the eye and should be used in these instances in conjunction with the remedy Ledum. Symphytum is the remedy to be given in fractures of the bone. The recommended potency would range from 5x or 6c to 30x or 30c.

▪ REMEDIES FOR SPECIFIC ▪ MEDICAL CONDITIONS

Colic (Digestive Disorders)

Nux vomica 30x This is the initial remedy to give when the first signs of indigestion and restlessness occur. It is a major remedy to consider in digestive disturbances. It is also an excellent remedy for constipation. Nux vomica has a very beneficial effect on the digestive system. In the initial stages of colic it can be given every half-hour for several doses until the condition subsides. If no improvement is seen after a few doses, consider another colic remedy.

Colocynthis 30x Colocynthis is one of the main remedies to consider in cases of spasmodic colic. The animal is in obvious discomfort and the colicky pains are paroxysmal. The horse will have a tendency to roll on the ground and arch his back. The horse is better when moving and worse after eating or drinking, although he may have no desire to eat. The 30x potency can be given at fifteen-minute intervals until relief occurs, and the dose can then be spread to hourly intervals until the horse is comfortable.

Colocynthis in the 1m potency would be indicated in very severe, acute cases. This potency would be administered often and decreased as the animal improves.

Colchicum 30x The horse tends to remain standing when this remedy is needed and there is much rumbling of gas in the abdomen. The abdomen appears distended, particularly the lower-right area. The horse may have an aversion to food and may resent being walked.

Aconite 30x This remedy can be given in the very early stages, one dose every fifteen minutes for one hour.

Diarrhea

Arsenicum album 1m The animal that needs the remedy Arsenicum album will show restlessness, anxiety, and thirst for small quantities of water frequently. The animal may be worse around midnight or 1 A.M. The skin may be dry with white flakes. The legs and ears may be cold and the stool can be watery with a cadaverous odor. The dose would be four times a day for a few days. Stop or decrease the dosage as the diarrhea decreases.

Nux vomica 30x This remedy is an excellent one for any digestive disorder. The remedy can be given three to four times a day.

China 30x An important remedy to give in cases of weakness due to loss of body fluids. It can be given after a bleeding episode or after loss of considerable fluid from diarrhea. This remedy would help build up the horse that has suffered from chronic diarrhea. The remedy can be given two to three times a day for a few days.

Podophyllum 30x The stool may be a light yellow or light brown color and is watery. This remedy is better suited for long-standing cases. The dose would be three times a day.

Colocynthis 30x The attack of diarrhea would be preceded and accompanied by severe abdominal pain. This remedy has been discussed under COLIC.

Mercurius corrosivus 30c When this remedy is indicated, the stool is often slimy and may contain mucus and/or blood. There may be straining even after the stool has passed.

Lycopodium 30c This is an excellent homeopathic remedy for chronic digestive disorders. The horse may resent being touched around the liver area. The horse may have an abnormal or a poor appetite. The animal may put his head in a corner and yawn a lot. Horses that yawn a lot are good subjects for liver remedies. In a chronic case, the remedy would be given once a day for a few weeks.

SKIN DISORDERS

Urticaria
This is an allergic condition of the skin where welts or wheals appear as circular puffy lesions on the skin. There are usually multiple lesions and the problem progresses rapidly.

Urtica urens 30x This remedy can be given every hour for four doses. It is the initial remedy to consider for this problem.

Apis 30x The plaques may be very large and puffy with a shiny reddish coloration. The condition is aggravated by heat and relieved by cold compresses.

Antimonium crudum 6c There are many itchy small plaques when this remedy is indicated.

Ringworm

Bacillinum 200c This remedy should be given in all cases of ringworm. The sclera or white of the eye can have a bluish tinge. The lesions are circular in pattern. This remedy would be given once or twice a week for a few weeks.

Tellurium 30c When the lesions are circular in shape and are distributed evenly on both sides of the body, this remedy can be useful. It should be given once a week for a few weeks.

Chrysarobinum 30c The ringworm can appear dry with crusts, and be itchy.

Psorinum 1m An excellent remedy for a horse with a chronic tendency toward skin problems. The animal may have a musty smell and an unhealthy-looking coat. The dosage would be twice a week for one month.

Sepia 30c This remedy may be indicated in ringworm. It is also a good remedy for reproductive problems.

Berberis vulgaris 30c This can also be indicated in ringworm.

Warts

Thuja 30c This remedy is excellent for warts in horses, particularly granulomatous warts on the inguinal region. Dose once a day for thirty days. Thuja tincture may also be applied topically to the wart.

MISCELLANEOUS

Shock

Aconite 30x or 1m Given every fifteen minutes for four doses.

Arnica 30x Given every hour for four doses.

Phosphorus 30c This remedy would be given in cases where the condition resulted from rapid loss of red blood. One or two doses are sufficient.

Carbo Vegetabilis 30c This remedy has been called the "corpse reviver." It is indicated when the body is cold and blue and breathing is shallow. The animal will be in an extreme state of collapse.

Dehydration

China 30x This is the best remedy for weakness due to loss of bodily fluids. It helps the body quickly restore itself to a healthy equilibrium. Give one dose three times a day for a few days.

Abscesses

Myristica 30x A remedy of great antiseptic powers, excellent to use for fistulas and abscesses. One dose three times a day until the abscess opens and drains is sufficient.

Hepar sulphuris 30x This remedy is good for abscesses that are very painful. The horse will exhibit great sensitivity to touch. This remedy can work in one of two ways. It can either open an abscess that is ready to drain or dissolve a small abscess that is still firm. It should be given every half-hour or hour for four to six doses.

Silicea 30x Has an excellent reputation for its ability to push foreign material from the body. It is commonly given to push splinters out of wounds. This remedy would not be indicated in a hot abscess, however; it is of greater benefit in the chronic and cold abscess. The pus may be creamy. It will encourage the body to push out the pus, promote healthy tissue growth, and decrease scarring. It can be given twice a day for a few days and then once a day until the abscess shows good signs of healing.

TOPICALLY: After they have opened, abscesses can also be rinsed with diluted Calendula and Hypericum tinctures. If you are using Hepar Sulph to treat an abscess that is just about to open, you can hot-pack it if the animal will allow.

Epistaxis (Nose Bleed)

Vipera 30c, 200c, or 1m This remedy should be tried first in any case of epistaxis. The lower potencies can be given once a day and the higher twice a week. Begin with the lower potencies and then change to the higher potencies after a week.

Crotalis 30c The blood is often dark-colored when this remedy is needed. It can be given three times a day for one week.

Phosphorus 30c This is an excellent remedy for nosebleeds in which the blood is bright red and fluid. It can be given two times a day for a few days and then once a day for a week or two.

Aconite, Arnica Should be given as immediate treatment for acute epistaxis. They both can be given every half-hour for two hours. The 30x potency can prove useful.

China Should be administered if the animal appears shaky from the blood loss. One or two doses is sufficient. The 30x potency can be used.

EYE PROBLEMS

General Remedies

Euphrasia Made from the herb eyebright, this is an excellent remedy to consider when the eye is inflamed and tearing. It can also be used as a wash by diluting the tincture 1:10 and flushing the eye. Both the oral remedy and the tincture can be used three times a day. The 30x potency is sufficient.

Phosphorus Phosphorus is an excellent remedy for all the structures of the eye. While Euphrasia works on the more superficial structures of the eye, Phosphorus works on the deeper ones. It can be used for cases of retinitis, glaucoma, iriditis, and conjunctivitis. The 30x potency can be administered two or three times a day.

Wounds of the Eye

Aconite, Arnica, Hypericum, and Ledum can be given orally, and a diluted rinse of Calendula and Hypericum can be used to irrigate the eye. Dilute the tinctures at least 1:10 for the eye.

Conjunctivitis

Aconite 30x This remedy would be given in the early stages of the condition in four doses over one hour.

Arnica 30x Given three times a day if the inflammation resulted from an injury to the eye.

Euphrasia 30x This remedy would be given in cases where the eye is tearing; the dose would be three times a day. The diluted tincture of Euphrasia can also be flushed in the eye at the same dosage rate.

Mercurius solubis 6c This remedy would be used if the discharge was purulent with a greenish coloration; dosed at a rate of three times a day.

Periodic Ophthalmia

This form of ophthalmia has a recurrent nature.

Phosphorus 6c This is an excellent remedy for this condition. Begin treatment with a 6c potency two times a day for one week and then go to the 1m potency twice a week for a month, then follow with once a week for a month.

Moon Blindness

Silicea 1m This is the indicated remedy for this recurrent inflammation. Give one dose twice a day for at least two weeks.

RESPIRATORY PROBLEMS

Influenza

Aconite 1m This remedy can be given every fifteen minutes for one hour in the initial stages only.

Belladonna 1m Indicated in cases in which a high fever comes on suddenly. There is a full, bounding pulse and the pupils are dilated. The horse feels very warm and is easily excited. Give one dose once an hour for four to six hours.

Bryonia 30x The horse is disinclined to move and has dry mucous membranes. He may have a cough and exhibit a thirst for large quantities of water. Begin at four times a day and increase potency if needed.

Phosphorus 30x The eyes may appear shiny and glazed. This horse may also be thirsty. The condition may appear to be degenerating into pneumonia. Begin at two times a day and increase potency if needed.

Gelsemium 200c The horse may appear drowsy and have a weakness in the muscles with some incoordination of movement. Three times a day.

Antimonium tartaricum 30x (also known as Cimifuga) Moist congestion is present in the chest. Two times a day.

Pneumonia

Phosphorus 1m or 10m This is a main remedy to use in the initial stages of pneumonia in the horse. One dose given two times in one hour may produce good results. If the pneumonia has progressed and the horse is beyond the acute state, give Phosphorus 30c four times a day for several days as improvement continues.

Many of the remedies listed above for influenza can be used with pneumonia if the modalities concur.

EQUINE LAMENESS: MUSCULOSKELETAL SYSTEM

Tendinitis

This is a manifestation of severe sprain or excessive physical stress. The tendon is swollen and painful. Examples of tendinitis are bowed tendons and constriction of the annular ligaments.

Tenosynovitis

Tenosynovitis is the inflammation and swelling of the synovial sheath that lubricates and surrounds a tendon. The swelling is often painless unless there is also a tendinitis. Examples of tenosynovitis are thoroughpin, bog spavin, windpuffs (windgalls).

Arnica 30x This remedy should be given as soon as possible after injury occurs. It can be given four times a day and can be given in conjunction with the following remedies if needed.

Ruta 30x An excellent remedy for any damage to tendons and ligaments. It can be given three times a day for one or two weeks and the potency can be increased to Ruta 1m if improvement is slow.

Rhus toxidendron 30x Rhus tox is indicated when the horse is better after slow motion. It is also an excellent remedy for inflammation of the tendons. The dosage can be the same as for Ruta.

Bryonia 30x If the horse is worse after movement and there is heat around the area, this remedy may prove useful. The horse will not resent gentle and firm pressure on the area, but there may be some tenderness around the joint.

Apis 30c If the horse has hot, puffy swellings and there is noticeable edema in the area, a few doses of Apis will reduce the swelling and heat.

Hypericum 30x This remedy should be given three times a day in cases of sprain of the sacroiliac joint.

EXTERNALLY: Arnica in an oil or salve applied locally to the area will assist in the healing process.

Bursitis

Situated between moving parts are slippery double layers of tissue called bursae. Occasionally, after repeated chronic injuries (such as sprains and bumps), a bursa becomes inflamed and swollen. The shoulder joint (bicipital bursitis), elbow joint, hock, or knee joint may become involved. Navicular disease is an inflammation of the bursa that helps to support the navicular bone. Navicular disease is perhaps the most common cause of intermittent front-leg lameness in the horse. The symptoms of navicular disease disappear with rest but always reappear on exercise. Other examples of bursitis are shoulder-joint bursitis, capped elbow, capped hock, capped knee, and whirl bone lameness.

Ruta graveolens 30x or 1m Tendons and muscles are injured when this remedy is required. Inflammation of the periosteum may be present. Give one dose three times a day for several days and then reduce the dose as improvement occurs.

Bryonia 30x, 30c, 200c, or 1m The horse will be worse after movement and improved upon resting. This remedy can be given two or three times a day and decreased with improvement. The potency may be increased if necessary.

Arnica 30x This remedy will assist in the healing of associated soft tissues. Give one dose three times a day.

Hypericum 30x Hypericum is a remedy that will work on damaged nerve endings and help to alleviate pain. Give one dose two to three times a day. A higher potency may be used if necessary.

Apis 30x This remedy is administered when synovitis of the bursa is suspected. There may be edema and heat and the discomfort may be relieved by cold compresses. Give one dose two to four times a day.

Chronic Navicular Disease

The remedies listed below are intended to help alleviate fibrous adhesions that develop in the bursa and any bony changes.

Calcarea fluorica 200c This remedy would be used in a case where bony changes are developing. Give one dose twice a week for six weeks.

Silicea 200c This remedy promotes strong healing and decreases fibrous-tissue formation. The dose would be once a day for seven days and then once a week for six weeks. Do not give this remedy and Calc fluor at the same time.

Joint Injuries

A joint injury is caused by stretching and injuring the joint capsule and its supporting ligaments, which can happen when movement is forced beyond its normal range. The ligaments of the knee, the suspensory ligament of the fetlock, the distal sesamoid ligaments, and the ligaments of the stifle joint are some of the ligaments that can be sprained.

Arnica 30x This remedy helps all musculoskeletal tissues to heal. One dose given three times a day for a few days is adequate.

Ruta graveolens 30x or 1m The remedy of choice for any damage to tendons and ligaments. Three times a day dosage will promote healing.

Rhus toxidendron 30x or 1m Rhus tox is also an excellent remedy for sprains and strains. It can be given routinely and is often needed when the animal is better after slow movement. Again, one dose three times a day will promote healing.

Symphytum 30x Helps to decrease the pain caused by the tearing of the periosteum that occurs in sprains. One dose two times a day for a week or two is adequate.

Bryonia 30x Bryonia would be indicated in cases where there is a concurrent synovitis with swelling and discomfort in the joint capsule. The horse will not resent a firm gentle pressure on the area but will be disinclined to move.

Silicea 30x This remedy, given twice a week, will help prevent the formation of scar tissue and reduce bony changes.

EXTERNALLY: Arnica and Ruta may be applied as a liniment or lotion.

Periostitis

The periosteum is a thick layer of connective tissue that wraps the bones. Inflammation of this area is called periostitis. Ligaments attach to the periosteum, and when a ligament is stretched or torn there is often concurrent damage to the periosteum. A direct injury to the bone such as a blow can also damage the periosteum. Some specific types of periostitis are bucked shins, splints, sesamoiditis, and ringbone.

Arnica 30x When there is swelling of the soft tissues present, this remedy can be given three times a day until the swelling subsides.

Ruta 30x or 1m Ruta is a most important remedy in sprains and damage to the periosteum. Give this remedy three times a day and decrease the dose as definitive improvement occurs. This will encourage quick healing.

Symphytum 30x Will rapidly promote healing in any type of injury to bone. Give this remedy at a rate of three times a day for a few days and then once a day for a week or two.

Rhus toxidendron 30x Rhus tox should be given for sprains and strains in horses. It is an excellent remedy for equine lameness in general and should always be used when the horse is stiffer after resting and better from movement.

Calcarea fluorica 200c Give this remedy twice a week for exostosis of the bone.

Silicea 30x This remedy at a dose of once a week will prevent scar tissue and decrease existing scar tissue.

Hypericum 30x Given three times a day, this remedy will alleviate pain in the nerve endings.

EXTERNALLY: A liniment of Ruta and Arnica will help.

Arthritis

The term *arthritis* denotes a number of joint diseases that are characterized by inflammation, degeneration, and new bone formation in and around the joints. *Serous arthritis* (sometimes called *acute synovitis*) denotes an acute reaction oftentimes due to trauma. *Infectious arthritis* occurs when bacteria from the bloodstream settle in the joints. *Degenerative joint disease* is the end result of the process and bony changes are present. Bone spavin is an example of degenerative arthritis of the hock joint.

Rhus toxidendron 1m This remedy is indicated when the animal stiffens up and is in more pain in damp wet weather and after rest. There is a marked increase in symptoms with cold weather. The horse is better after mild exercise. Rhus tox 1m can be given once a day for one week, and if improvement occurs, the dosage can be decreased. Rhus tox 30c, 30x, or 200c can be given routinely at a dose of once a day for chronic stiffness with arthritis. It is one of the best arthritis remedies for the horse.

Bryonia 30c or 200c This remedy is indicated in arthritis cases in which the horse is better after resting. It can be dosed at once or twice a day as needed. Pressure over the joints relieves the symptoms.

Ruta, Symphytum, and *Arnica* can be given in conjunction with one of the above remedies to assist in the healing of the injured tissues and bone.

EQUINE LAMENESS: THE FOOT

Puncture Wounds and Abscesses

Ledum 30x Should be given for all puncture wounds at a dose of three times a day for two days.

Hypericum 30x Indicated for puncture wounds and for all injuries to nerve endings. The dose would be three times a day for a few days.

Myristica 30x An important remedy for abscesses of the foot. It can be used for any abscess and often works well on very deep abscesses. A dose of three times a day until the abscess is drained and healed is suggested.

Hepar sulphurica 30c This remedy is indicated for very painful abscesses of the hoof in which the horse resents any pressure. The dose would be three to four times a day until the abscess opens and drains.

Silicea 30x Silicea is an excellent remedy to help reduce scar tissue and is also indicated for cold abscesses. One or two doses a few days apart to decrease scarring, and once a day for an abscess, is sufficient.

Calcarea sulphurica 30x This remedy can be given after an abscess has opened to promote draining and healing. Twice a day for a few days is an adequate dose.

Corns

Silicea 30x Silicea would be used in supportive corns (corns that have pus) and will help to control infection. Give it once a day for two weeks.

Calcarea fluorica 200x Given twice a week, it will help to absorb the hard tissue.

Thrush

In this condition, a black necrotic material accumulates in the grooves of the frog of the foot. Unsanitary stable conditions contribute to the occurrence of thrush.

Kreosotum 200c This is the main remedy to consider in

cases of thrush. It can be given once or twice a day for one or two weeks.

Silicea 30x Will help the diseased tissue to heal and promote strong restructuring of the new tissue.

The frog of the foot can be packed with a dressing soaked in Calendula and Arnica once a day to promote healing.

Brittle Hooves, Sandcrack
Silicea 200c Given at a dose of three times a week, this remedy will promote healing and strong hard hooves.

Acute Founder—Laminitis
Crotalis 10m This remedy will act on the vasoconstricted area. Crotalis horridus is prepared as a homeopathic remedy from rattlesnake venom. It acts on the vascular system. Give Crotalis 10m two times a day for five days and follow it with the remedy Secale.

Secale 6c This remedy aids normal circulation to the feet. It should follow Crotalis and be given every other day for one month.

Belladonna 1m Belladonna would be administered initially when the horse is restless, sweating, and exhibiting a full and bounding pulse. There may be fever present. Give it every half-hour for four doses and then one dose an hour after the last one, five doses in all.

Aconite 1m Aconite can be administered immediately after the first symptoms are noted. One dose should be given every fifteen minutes for four doses.

Chronic Founder—Laminitis
Rhus toxidendron 1m Give once a day for two weeks and then every other day for one month.

Calcarea fluorica 200c This remedy will help prevent tissue destruction and scarring and can be given twice a week for one month.

NERVOUS SYSTEM DISORDERS

Wobbler Syndrome (Cervical Vertebral Malformation)

Wobbling is the most frequently seen neurological disease in the horse. Symptoms can include hind-limb incoordination, weakness, ataxia, lowered head carriage, and a swinging gait. It is caused by pressure on the spinal column resulting from a narrowing of the vertebral canal.

Helleborus niger 30c, 200c This remedy acts primarily on the cerebrospinal system and the spinal cord. The horse will exhibit muscular weakness and a wobbly gait. The animal may appear listless and have trouble starting and stopping when walking. Give one dose three times a day and go up in potency if needed.

Gelsemium 200c The horse that needs Gelsemium may exhibit some trembling of the muscles. The horse may tire easily. Give this remedy three times a day for a week and continue if necessary.

Hypericum and Ruta 30c Given three times a day, these remedies will aid the healing process.

Conium 30c An excellent remedy for paralysis, particularly ascending paralysis. It can work very well when the potency is increased over time. Conium 30c can be given three times a day for a few days, then Conium 200c can be given twice a day, followed by Conium 1m and so on.

Paralysis of the Facial Nerve

Hypericum 30x An excellent remedy for nerve injuries. Dose at three times a day.

Gelsemium 30x Very helpful for paralysis of specific groups of nerves, especially around the head area. It is a remedy to consider in paralysis of motor nerves, particularly after infection. Begin with Gelsemium 30x at a dose of three times a day for a few days and go to a higher potency later if no improvement occurs with the lower potency.

Causticum 30x A good remedy to use with paralysis of isolated areas, particularly the face, larynx, and sphincters. It is good for paralytic weakness of the urinary bladder. This remedy is indicated in conditions that have arisen due to exposure to cold.

Paralysis of the Femoral Nerve or Radial Nerve
The same remedies as used in paralysis of the facial nerve may be indicated, with the addition of:

Plumbum 30c When this remedy is indicated the reflexes are often lost. Give one dose twice a day for one week.

Curare 30c With this remedy, weakness of muscles is often associated with trembling. Dose at three times a day for one week.

• CONCLUSION •

Only the very basic remedies for treating the more common ailments seen in horses have been mentioned here. A reading list will be found at the end of this chapter that provides more information. It is advisable to maintain a homeopathic kit with the more common remedies for the kinds of problems you often encounter in your barn, since medical problems that are treated promptly often resolve themselves more quickly. These remedies should in no way replace regular veterinary diagnosis and care of your horse.

Many of the therapies mentioned in this book work together in a complementary fashion. For example, for a horse with wobbles or nerve paralysis, treatment by a qualified veterinary acupuncturist as well as with homeopathic remedies is well advised. I hope you enjoy the results of these marvelous remedies as much as I do.

LIST OF HOMEOPATHIC PHARMACIES

BHI
11600 Cochiti South East
Albuquerque, NM 87123
505-293-3843

Boericke and Tafel
1011 Arch Street
Philadelphia, PA 19107
215-922-2967

Boiron Borneman
1208 Amostand Road
Box 54
Norwood, PA 19074
215-532-2035

Celletech Ltd.
518 Tasman St., Suite C
Madison, WI 53714
608-221-9412

Dolisos America Inc.
3014 Rigel Street
Las Vegas, NV 89102
800-824-8455

Humphreys Pharmacal
63 Meadow Road
Box 256
Rutherford, NJ 07070
201-933-7744

Luyties Pharmacal
4200 Laclede Avenue
St. Louis, MO 63108
800-325-8080

Standard Homeopathic
210 W. 131st Street
Box 61067
Los Angeles, CA 90061
213-627-1555

Weleda
841 South Main Street
Spring Valley, NY 10977
914-352-6145

▪ BIBLIOGRAPHY ▪

VETERINARY HOMEOPATHY

MacLeod, George. *Cats: Homeopathic Remedies*. Great Britain, 1990. Written by one of the foremost authorities on the homeopathic treatment of animals, this book lists the common illnesses of cats with the suggested remedy and potency for treatment. It also contains a short materia medica of these common remedies.

———. *Dogs: Homeopathic Remedies*. Great Britain, 1983; reprint, 1989.

———. *The Treatment of Cattle by Homeopathy*. Great Britain, 1981.

———. *Treatment of Horses by Homeopathy*. Great Britain, 1977; reprint 1984.

———. *A Veterinary Materia Medica and Clinical Repertory with a Materia Medica of the Nosodes*. Great Britain, 1983.

Pitcairn, Richard, and Susan Pitcairn. *Dr. Pitcairn's Complete Guide to Natural Health for Dogs and Cats*. United States, 1977; reprint, 1982.

Shepherd, K. *Homeopathic Treatment of Cats*. Great Britain, 1960; reprint, 1981.

———. *Treatment of Dogs by Homeopathy*. Great Britain, 1963; reprint, 1983.

Wolff, H. G. *Your Healthy Cat: Homeopathic Medicines for Common Feline Ailments*. United States, 1991. Describes how to treat many common acute and chronic ailments in cats, including problems in the ear, nose, and throat; the heart and circulatory system; the digestive organs; the ligaments, tendons, and joints; the reproductive system and urinary tract; and the skin.

DISCOVERING HOMEOPATHY

Aubin, Michel, and Philippe Picard. *Homeopathy—A Different Way of Treating Common Ailments*. Great Britain, 1986; reprint, 1989. Two French doctors describe their research, their view of homeopathy, and how the remedies are made, and give examples of how homeopathy worked when other methods did not. Also includes homeopathic first aid.

————. *What is Homeopathy?* France, 1982; reprint 1986. A 16-page pamphlet that details basic information on the science and practice of homeopathy. Good bibliography.

Boiron. *Pocket Guide To Homeopathy*. France, 1986. The perfect "little book" (32 pages) for the individual with little or no knowledge of homeopathy. Explains the underlying principles and virtues of the homeopathic approach to medicine.

Clarke, John. *Prescriber*. Great Britain, 1972; reprint, 1983. Alphabetical presentation of a select group of conditions with their corresponding homeopathic remedies. A good introductory intermediate text.

Garrett, Raymond J., and TaRessa Stone. *Catching Good Health with Homeopathic Medicine*. United States, 1987; reprint, 1990. A concise, self-help introduction to homeopathy which explains what it is, how to use it at home, examples of cures, where to buy the medicines and how to find a homeopathic doctor.

Handley, Rima. *A Homeopathic Love Story*. United States, 1990. A myth-destroying account of the romance of Samuel Hahnemann and Melanie, plus invaluable information on Hahnemann's homeopathic practice.

Shadman, Alonzo. *Who Is Your Doctor and Why?* United States, 1958; reprint, 1980.

Shepherd, Dorothy. *Homeopathy for the First Aider.* Great Britain, 1982.

Smith, Trevor. *Homeopathic Medicine: A Dr.'s Guide to Remedies for Common Ailments.* Great Britain, 1983.

Speight, Phyllis. *A Study Course in Homeopathy.* Great Britain, 1988. Twelve lessons lead the student from a knowledge of the basic principles of homeopathy to an understanding of their application to acute and chronic afflictions. Some of the most important homeopathic remedies are outlined. Case-taking and suggestions for questioning the patient are detailed.

Ullman, Dana. *Discovering Homeopathy: Medicine for the 21st Century.* United States, 1988. Ullman is the ultimate skeptic convincer. An introductory book that describes principles, history, research, and various applications of homeopathy in clinical practice; brings a modern freshness and insight into homeopathy.

Vithoulkas, George. *Homeopathy: Medicine of the New Man.* United States, 1979.

MATERIA MEDICA

Boericke, William. *Materia Medica.* United States, 1927; reprint, 1984. The fundamental required text for the practice of homeopathy; provides an alphabetical listing of remedies along with characteristics and pathology.

Clarke, John. *Dictionary of Practical Materia Medica*, 3 vols. India, 1978; reprint, 1990.

Gibson, Douglas. *Studies of Homeopathic Remedies.* Great Britain, 1987. An alphabetical list of remedies with a wide range of insights on each remedy. This text is of great practical value to the homeopathic clinician.

Jouanny, Jacques. *Essentials of Homeopathic Materia Medica*. Francc, 1980. An incisive, in-depth view of a selected group of homeopathic remedies including their complete pathology and keys to utility. The most up-to-date materia medica available, a companion volume to *Essentials of Homeopathic Therapeutics*.

Kent, James. *Lectures on Homeopathic Materia Medica*. India, 1984.

MASSAGE

CRAIG DENEGA

INTRODUCTION

Massage is an ancient art. It is purposeful manipulation of muscle, sinew, and joints in order to increase range of motion, elasticity, and circulation within tissue, while gradually expanding the limits of accommodation. It involves using the interaction of two living beings to produce a specific or desired effect upon one of the beings, without diminishing the well-being of the other. Massage also gives special attention to areas where the subject is feeling pain in order to promote the creation and circulation of the body's innate restorative materials. This is accomplished by applying pressure on the control mechanisms (acu-points), by stimulation of the organs themselves, and by promoting intercellular communication whereby the innate wisdom of the body is mobilized to correct deficiencies. Finally, massage loosens the constrictive bonds of physical tension (undirected energy) that impede the flow of motion.

Massage undoubtedly existed before the written word and well before mankind had even rudimentary tools to attempt dissections in order to view the inner complexities of the body. Cave paintings in the Pyrenees dating back over 15,000 years and ancient rock carvings in China, Tibet, India, and Egypt bear testimony to how long mankind has used massage therapy.

Yet massage has been perhaps the most understated, unknown, and misunderstood of all the healing arts. It is based more on observations, interactions, and successive approximations than on any strictly adhered to formulas. Massage is one of the five basic facets of traditional Chinese medicine, a body of knowledge nearly 5,000 years old whose wisdom is just beginning to be understood today in the West. The Chinese and other ancient cultures teach that life must be lived in balance. They place emphasis on proper use of food, on balancing exercises for the body (Yoga, gymnastics), on centering exercises for the mind (meditation, mathematics), and on attainment of the spiritual way of harmony. Massage, acupuncture, herbs, and lately chiropractic are used to gently assist in the physical balancing process. By relieving the bonds of the physical, the mind and spirit are refreshed and released to pursue higher goals. Holistic theory holds that all "dis-ease" comes from a prolonged exposure to an imbalance or ambivalence among mind, body, spirit, and emotions.

Western culture to some extent acknowledges the importance of massage and touch as part of a healing process. The Hippocratic Oath states in part, "I will never forget the Art of Massage, nor He who taught me the Art." Ancient religions abound in references to the healing power of the "laying on of hands."

In this century, massage was administered by nurses in the military until medical interventions were deemed faster and cheaper. As modern man's ability to cause severe bodily trauma has been perfected, so modern medicine has had to keep pace with more devastating injuries. Overlooked, however, are the insidious, slowly progressing infirmities that eventually debilitate. Often they are connected with one's occupation, and athletes—whether human or equine—are among those at greatest risk.

• WHEN *NOT* TO MASSAGE •

Pain is the body's way of alerting the sufferer that something is wrong. It is an indication that all is not well within the system, and that one should slow down before further injury results. Usually, the more persistent and painful the alert, the more serious the situation. A quick pain or a sore ache during a particular movement may be compensated for or ignored, but a searing, constant internal pain cannot be ignored; it may be indicative of a life-threatening condition. *The latter should be addressed by a physician.* Massage is ideally suited to the former condition; it offers a gentle, progressive relief, especially useful in smoothing out old muscle injuries that inhibit free motion. Massage is at its best as a prophylactic treatment to ensure continuous health and well-being. When combined with sensible exercise and a nutritious diet, it can prolong optimum physical efficiency.

• THE CAUSES OF MUSCLE DAMAGE •

Muscles become intractable as a result of: injury (a blow), overuse, overstretching (a tear), cooling down too fast—(especially after overheating), postural imbalance (incorrect shoes), structural imbalance, fever, disease, systemic imbalance, poor diet, even sluggish liver function. Maximum possible physical effort will damage muscles, and chances of injury increase dramatically during the demands of competition, especially if the muscles are not properly warmed up. Since a muscle responds to stress or injury by contracting, it can put uneven or unnecessary stress on either a joint or on the opposing muscle. That causes friction, heat, uneven wear, limited range of motion, and possibly compensatory efforts from all of the other muscles, resulting in excessive expenditure of energy even when at rest. The job of the massage practitioner is to find, through sense and touch, these "damaged" areas, which I will call "knurdles," and restore them to normal functioning.[1]

• THE IMPORTANCE OF TOUCH •

Studies have indicated that touch is important to normal development and that lack of touch may lead to aggressive tendencies and violent behavior. Underdeveloped babies respond dramatically to touch. Prisoners are punished most severely by being put into solitary confinement.

The skin is the largest organ of the body, and indications are that the first sense that develops is the "sense of touch." Reaction to stimuli is one of the best indications that an animal is alive. The art of massage is a further development and refinement of touch in order to achieve a desired physical effect.

Massage for horses likewise has been applied in various forms for many years. Animals respond to touch, food, and kindness, all of which play an important part in what we call domestication. From modern records alone, there are reports of 1850s cavalrymen using horse massage. Turn-of-the-century European grooms described rubbing horses, "the old way." Jack Meagher, the "Father of Sportsmassage," and others have been practicing horse massage in the United States for years. For a common thought or technique of rejuvenation to be carried through all of these cultures for all of these years, there must be something to it!

• WHAT MASSAGE CAN DO •

Massage does not attempt to cure anything. It allows and encourages the body to heal itself. Massage has been shown to:

- improve circulation and dilate blood vessels.

- increase the number of red blood cells.

- stimulate lymph circulation.

- hasten elimination of wastes and toxic debris.

- relax spastic muscles.

- relieve tension.

- increase nutrition to the tissues by improving general circulation (increases interchange of substances between the blood and tissue cells, heightening tissue metabolism).

- increase the excretion (via the kidneys) of fluids, inorganic phosphorus, salts, and the waste products of protein metabolism.

- lengthen connective tissue (improves its circulation and nutrition and so breaks down or prevents the formation of adhesions and reduces the danger of fibrosis).

- improve the circulation and nutrition of joints and hasten the elimination of harmful deposits.

- help lessen inflammation and swelling in joints and so alleviate pain.

- increase blood supply and nutrition to muscles without adding to their load of toxic lactic acid produced through voluntary muscle contraction (massage thus helps to prevent buildup of harmful "fatigue" products, metabolic wastes, and lactic acid resulting from strenuous exercise, by promoting cellular exchange).

- enhance muscle tone and increase range of motion and generally improve the disposition, as it relieves discomfort.

Through the deliberate manipulation of the surface muscles and fasciae, massage endeavors to free motion throughout the body and to correct damaged muscles by releasing adhesions. "Any excess degree of muscle tightness, any spasm, adhesion, etc., that interferes with the free flow of oxygen into tissue and the flow of toxins out of the tissues, must have its effect upon total performance."[2] An additional benefit of massage is to stimulate the internal organs to do their job more efficiently and with less stress. If we can increase the ease of motion and decrease energy expenditure, we will have a happy animal, more than willing to try whatever is asked, for a long time.

• PAIN AND MASSAGE •

Pain is nature's way of telling us to "slow down"! Most pains are readily apparent, but there is also pain that doesn't announce itself until (or after) a person attempts to assume a certain position (say, a Yoga posture) or engages in a strenuous activity (like weekend touch football). In addition, there are old injuries that the body compensates for, that are noticed only at specific times, for example, when the weather changes, or when the areas are pressed or rubbed during massage. Massage need not be painful. Ideally, firm pressure is well received almost anywhere on the body—except at a few very obvious spots such as the eyes and throat. Otherwise, when there is pain, massage does not create the pain, it merely brings it to attention. When we use thumb pressure, for instance, we use only twelve to sixteen pounds of pressure, *gradually* exerted and released. The body abhors sudden changes in pressure, but if you depress and release rhythmically, a tolerance develops and the pain response diminishes. A deep-sea diver can tolerate tremendous amounts of pressure, but it cannot be released suddenly; if it is, the diver gets the bends and must immediately be repressurized. In the same way, if you hit your finger with a hammer, your instinct is to grab the finger and squeeze; by repressurizing and slowly releasing it, you find the injury far less traumatic. A "healthy" muscle feels good when touched. An injury sends pain messages.

In my twenty-plus years of massage experience, I have yet to find anyone who does not have his or her own Achilles' heel! Most learn to live with it, to accept the limitation. But that need not be the case, as those who have tried massage can attest. Massage has various effects, and most of them are imperceptibly subtle and gradual. Improvement with massage may seem slow, but the effects over time make it worth the patience and effort.

A word here about stretching. Slowly stretching the extremities through the full possible range of motion gives a good indication of the condition of the muscles involved in the release process. As with massage, stretching too fast is very painful, and it is dangerous as well, since it can cause debilitating injuries. Either modality, however, when done gradually, will release tight muscles and free the entire range of motion. By combining massage with stretching, you achieve a boost in circulation, a decrease of constrictions, and an increase in range of motion, so this combination is a valuable tool for injury prevention and maintenance.

• HOW TO MASSAGE YOUR HORSE •

In order for you to enjoy giving your horse a massage as much as the animal enjoys receiving it, you must learn to work smart!

First of all, use your weight, skeleton, and body leverage rather than trying to use your strength alone. You won't tire as quickly and will have more control. If your arms are bent, you are using muscle power; if they are straight, you're using proper body mechanics. Ideally, you should have a certain amount of muscle strength to begin

The proper dress and tools should consist of a hat to protect the face and ears from being nipped; a stable jacket that is too slippery for the horse to grab hold of; gloves with the fingertips removed for sensitivity; and heavy boots to protect the toes. (Steel-toe boots are not recommended because if they are stepped on hard enough to bend, they might be difficult to get off.)

with, and the more you practice, the faster it will develop. Don't get discouraged in the beginning. Learning becomes a series of approximations, reinforced by results. If your thumbs or fingertips get tired, use an elbow or knuckle. At times you may want to brace your arm against your hip and lean into the animal for added pressure. Often it is helpful to stand the animal against a wall in the stall, or against the fence in a pasture. If you know the animal and it is fairly quiet, you can stand next to and slightly above it on a hay bale to increase your leverage. If your arms are straight, and you are leaning into the animal, you can position yourself out of range of a "cow-kick."

SAFETY TIPS

Whenever I am working around the hind end, I *always* keep my free hand resting firmly against the horse's stifle, and stand to the side. Horses have tremendous strength aft, but it is fairly easy to block them from lifting or swinging a leg sideways. If you feel sideward contraction and push back, they can only kick out straight behind. Just make sure that there is nothing close behind. If you must stand behind a horse, it is a good idea to put a bale of hay (or a stack of two) at his feet to absorb any misdirected aggressions. Another ploy is to have someone hold up a foreleg on the same side you are working on. This is not foolproof, however; I've seen horses cow-kick quite gracefully with two legs on the ground! You will not enjoy giving a massage if you are nursing an injury of your own.

Make sure that you have an escape route mapped out if the horse should become startled or unmanageable. Avoid letting the horse get between you and the door.

When working on the shoulders, if you rest the hand closest to the horse's head high on his neck, you can prevent him from turning around enough to nip you by pushing back when he starts to turn his head. Wear loose clothing and a hat. That way if the horse does nip at you, you may lose some cloth instead of skin.

I have also been told, and have no experience to the contrary, that a horse must shift backward in order to rear up. If you have any reason to expect that the horse may try this, keep his hindquarters tightly in a corner.

Always speak soothingly while you are working, and reassure the horse periodically. Anticipate any misbehaviors and correct the horse vocally the first time, more adamantly the second time. A third instance calls for immediate discipline. But take it easy. Horses are large animals but very sensitive, and you don't want to provoke a reaction from pain. By following this advice, you will minimize your chances of getting hurt. If the horse is very touchy, try again later, or the next day. In fact, it is a good idea to wait a day or two between massage sessions to allow the horse's body to process the resulting changes.

Finally, with a horse that strongly resists, you may want to consult a veterinarian about tranquilizing the animal. But use this option only as a last resort! Unless you're dealing with a wild stallion, you should be able to finesse your way around the animal, by working gradually, by varying your strokes and pressures. Work on a spot for a few minutes, then go on to another for a few minutes. When you return to the original spot some of the sensitivity will have diminished. Tranquilizers inhibit true feedback from the animal. This makes it harder to tell just how sensitive particular spots really are, and as a result you could make the horse more sore than he was to begin with. Think of massage as exposure to the sun. It is comforting and nice, but it must be received in judicious doses at first. If one persists just a little too long, the resulting pain negates any previously perceived benefits.

"KNURDLES"

"Knurdle" is my word for a muscle that feels different from surrounding muscles. A "healthy" muscle, when it is not under contraction, is soft and yielding. Bend your arm to 90 degrees and rest it on something; now feel your biceps—up, down, and across. Are they soft and flaccid? Now "make a muscle" and run your fingers across it; feel the wire-like definition underneath. This is approximately what a knurdle feels like, although a true knurdle is accompanied by a pain reflex response. What you are feeling for is a muscle under involuntary contraction. A muscle can sustain only a given amount of tension, then it tries to release. An injury to the muscle can result in sustained contraction, so that the muscle cannot release. Soon cellular nutrients cease flowing freely through the muscle and it goes into a minor form of suffocation—panic, if you will—and like a drowning swimmer it grabs hold with what strength it has left and won't let go. This is the kind of spasm commonly referred to as a "charley horse." Massage attempts to resuscitate the muscle externally by repeated compression and release in order to spread the fibers. Compressing and spreading the muscle fibers increases the flow of nutrients and relieves the panic; the muscle begins to relax. Once the muscle begins to let go, continuing pressure forces out the "used" blood (full of metabolic wastes) and allows "fresh" blood into the tissue.

Sometimes knurdles can be found at the intersection of two muscles. Muscles are covered by a sheath that allows them to slide freely over each other. It sometimes happens that a "short circuit" develops between the muscles, so that the signal to contract "bleeds" from one muscle into the adjacent muscle, causing it to contract or lock up. In this case we use the accepted Red Cross method of direct pressure to stop the "bleeding." Gradually increase pressure, sustain for about thirty seconds, and then release slowly. The second time you apply pressure, slowly and

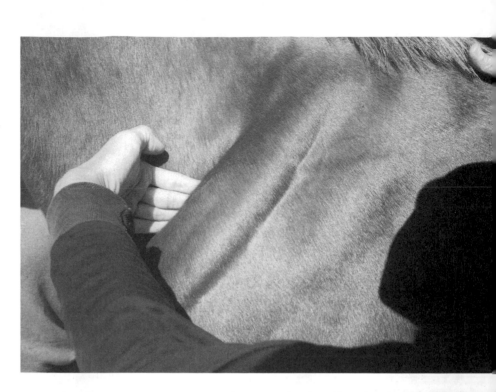

These pictures illustrate the pliability of "normal" muscles. *Above:* In this area they should be soft and allow entrance of the fingertips as shown. Do not confuse tight muscles and "fit" muscles. They are not the same! *Right:* This area is usually sensitive on riding horses. Move slowly. Usually if the animal is sensitive in the "armpit" he also will be touchy in the withers.

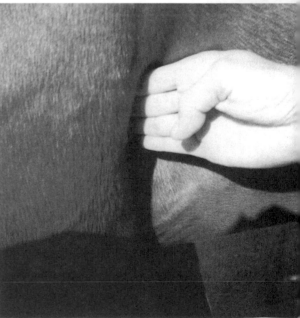

almost imperceptibly begin a very small circular motion as if to coax the muscles gently apart. If they have been attached for a long time, you cannot expect to get results all at once.

There is another kind of knurdle that is caused by a blow (compression) or a tear (decompression). If it is fresh, it may feel like a void or hole. Ice should be used to slow down the swelling. If it is an old injury, you may feel a tiny spot like a small lump in the muscle. Muscle fibers contract longitudinally, and for this we use "cross-fiber friction." These terms will be explained later in this chapter. Taking your cues from the horse as to how much he will tolerate, use firm pressure to compress the skin and rub crosswise along the length of muscle. *Do not* slip over the skin and cause a rub burn, but take the skin with you as far as it will go and press slowly back and forth for a while. Persevere until you can feel the spot beginning to soften, or until the horse objects. Remember, this is a painful area, so proceed gently! Put yourself in the horse's "shoes."

• PREPARING YOURSELF •

All this may sound a little complicated and daunting. I have three suggestions for getting past the strangeness you may feel at first about massaging horses.

My first recommendation is this: Find a massage practitioner with experience in either Sports Massage, acupressure, or any other of the deep-tissue modalities and have a session yourself! This will demonstrate at first "hand" how small changes in pressure and location can make a tremendous difference in sensations and results. You will also feel areas in your body that are sensitive that perhaps you never knew existed.

Second, I recommend that you first practice on a willing friend so that he or she can give you feedback. You need to develop a sense of what the horse may be feeling while you are working on it, and a friend can help by describing the sensations produced by your massage actions.

My third recommendation is that you always consider your personal safety! Before you begin—especially at first and if the horse is not your own—have the owner, trainer, or handler who is familiar with the animal present. This person can warn you of its idiosyncrasies and soothe the animal if it becomes nervous at the beginning. If you have any questions or doubts about the animal's overall physical condition, have a veterinarian check it out.

Now that you have some idea of what it is we're looking for, let's find a horse and practice!

▪ THE TECHNIQUES ▪ OF SPORTS MASSAGE ▪

When administering a massage to a horse, think of yourself as a skilled craftsman who is restoring a fine mansion to its former splendor. The more attention you place upon preserving the original details, the more rewarding will be the outcome. Don't rush! If you allow roughly one hour per horse, and divide the horse into three sections per side (head/neck/chest; withers/shoulder/leg; back/rump/leg/tail), you can go completely around the horse twice (at five minutes per section) in an hour. On the first go-around, you become acquainted and familiar with the animal. You will use the techniques of compression, jostling, percussion, direct pressure, and cross-fiber friction. Let me now explain these terms.

COMPRESSION

The basic stroke that makes sports massage different from other types of massage is compression. When the muscle is compressed against the bone, the muscle fibers spread apart, freeing restrictions and adhesions and allowing blood to flow easily into the muscle to deliver oxygen and nutrients and remove metabolic wastes. The muscle behaves as if it were "working" but it is burning much less energy.

Compression is used to break up adhesions in the "bellies" of the muscles and has no significant benefit for ten-

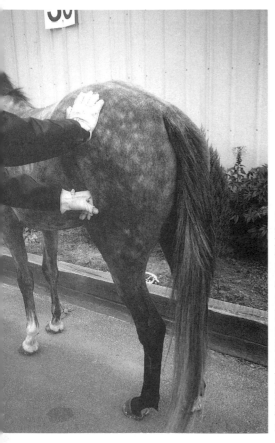

Use a loose fist to massage the hind leg (stifle). Here the right hand is used for pressure and protection. With the hand in this position, the horse can only kick to the rear. Keep your arm straight. If the horse attempts a side kick, the motion will push you away instead and you have some control over the direction that the hoof takes. The right hand feels for contractions that precede a kick and also reassures the animal.

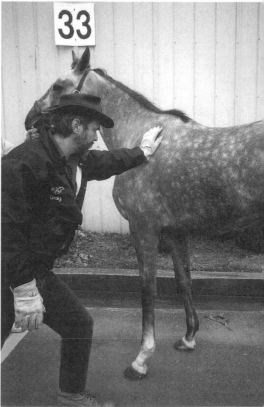

Compression with palms. Note the straight arms. Pressure is spread over a larger surface area, so you must compensate by leaning into the horse. Establish a rhythmic rocking motion. If the animal starts leaning back toward you, it means that he enjoys the pressure. Slowly rock and release, repositioning your working hand each time on the release. A slight twist may be imparted to your palm as you extend as you might do turning a key in a lock.

dons or ligaments. (These respond more to cross-fiber friction.) Compression can be done using the forearms, heel of the hand, or the knuckles of a loosely held fist.[3] Generally it is used to soften up large areas, unspecifically. Use a straight arm, and as you extend from the shoulder, rotate your elbow slightly. This will impart a gentle twisting motion to your hand that is useful in spreading apart muscle fibers. Encourage a cooperative motion from the horse. Remember to work rhythmically, and be sure to cover every square inch of the horse several times. Maintain an average pressure all around and see which areas provoke the most reaction. Moderate your pressure to your horse's tolerance. Each horse will be different and each stress point or muscle on a horse will be different. While the

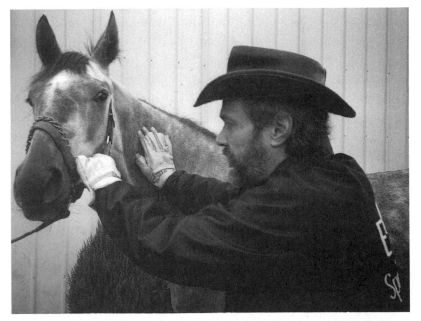

Jostling of the neck. The right hand pushes and the left hand pulls in a rocking, swaying motion. Establish a rhythm and gradually rock harder each time, feeling for the muscle relaxing under your right hand.

breaking up of spasms is painful, the general massage should not cause your horse to tense up under your hands. With compression, you can apply force without causing too much pain or discomfort.

JOSTLING

Jostling (shaking, rocking) is used most easily on the neck and shoulders, or where you can lift and shake the extremity or joint, allowing the muscle or joint to flop loosely. This can release tension and prepare the body for compression. But jostling is not as effective as compression in spreading the muscle fibers and increasing blood supply.

The procedure is much as the name implies. Stand to one side and begin gently rocking, using straight arms, against the horse. Think of making it a game, and see if the horse responds by leaning back into your weight. Adjust your rhythm to try to move as one. Move slowly around the entire body. Are the withers sensitive? Does the neck respond evenly along the entire length? Does the weight shift evenly as you work your way around? Is the horse always resting one leg? Make mental notes.

PERCUSSION

Excessive sensitivity is sometimes relieved by percussion. This stroke is always directed inward but stops at the skin surface, without a follow-through; it is *never* applied to an area that is not supported with skeletal structure, such as the abdominal cavity. Percussion is never applied directly over bone such as the shinbone, spinal column, or iliac crest. *Do not strike over the kidney area!* Percussion can be a light tapping with fingertips, a gentle striking with the outside edge of the palm (with loose fingers), or light

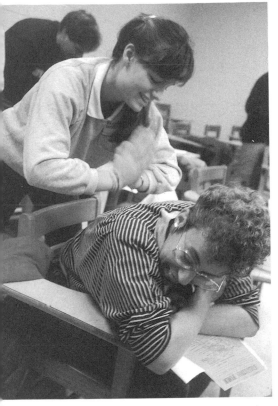

Percussion techniques. *Left:* Practice percussion on a friend. The idea is to press both your palms and fingers together, concentrating on keeping your fingers spread apart as far as possible. Lock your hands with your thumbs. Rotate from your forearms and strike with the edge of your hands. Practice until you determine the appropriate pressure. *Bottom Left:* Do the same to the horse. Using this technique it is almost impossible to hurt the horse without hurting yourself. *Bottom Right:* Use a closed fist. Move around, don't strike the same spot too often or it will get sore. Speak reassuringly to the horse while you do this to avoid giving the impression that discipline or commands are intended.

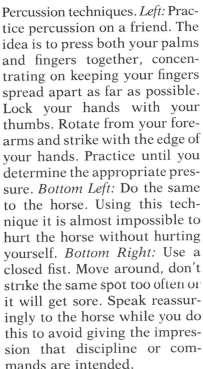

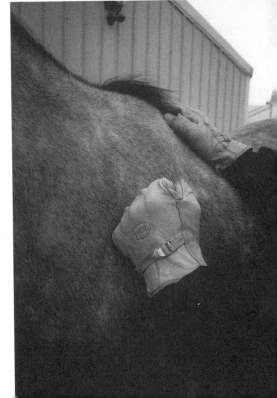

pounding with the sides of fists for denser muscles like the gluteals. Again, cover the area a section at a time, and feel the changes in resilience and reactions as you move slowly around.

DIRECT PRESSURE

Direct pressure is the key to efficiently eliminating muscle problems. You must work very slowly when you use concentrated pressure. Feel for a slippery, lumpy textured band or ball that "twangs" as you slip off of it. Maintain balanced pressure directly over the slippery (or, perhaps crunchy) spot, for at least thirty seconds.[4] Repeat this several times, and if your fingers tire, use your thumb, knuckle, or an elbow with your hand braced against your hip. Get comfortable and take a while. Don't hurry!

CROSS-FIBER FRICTION

The secret to breaking up muscle adhesions is cross-fiber friction. The technique is similar to direct pressure, but friction is applied transversely to the direction of the muscle fibers. Use your palms or fingers. Pressure is applied and maintained, then moved slowly across the muscle fibers. Moving too fast will result in a pain response.

If an injury site is too painful to touch, work the area around it. Include the rest of the entire muscle in order to relieve tension on the injured area. Most injuries occur at the musculotendinous junction. This is where the flexibility of the muscle ends and the less flexible tendon starts. It will be easier to locate stress points if you keep this in mind.

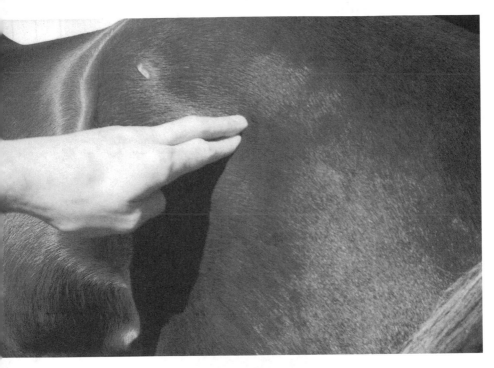

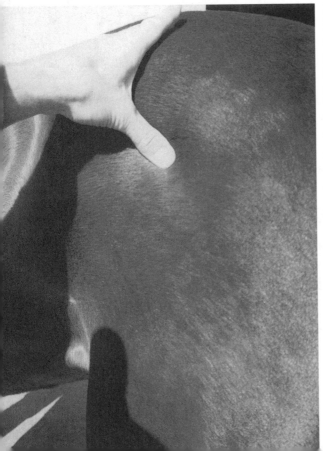

Direct pressure. *Above:* Using braced fingers takes some practice. This technique should be used sparingly and never where a sudden movement could "jam" your fingers. *Left:* Using the thumb. This will be extremely uncomfortable for the horse, so apply and release pressure gradually and move slowly. You may also hold until you feel a "softening" of the muscles. This thumb action, combined with an imperceptible circling motion, is *very* effective on knurdles.

Finger pressure directly on poll. The horse should gradually lower his nose to the ground. Feel for knurdles and press the center of them; you may have to switch hands or sides. Use your thumb on larger knurdles. When the horse lifts his head, it should be with the "chin toward chest." Maintain pressure. For this maneuver, a carrot may be used as an inducement to tease the head down. Move very slowly if the horse is known to be "head-shy" and you will probably find a rather large knurdle. *Note:* Use your free hand on the bridle as a guide.

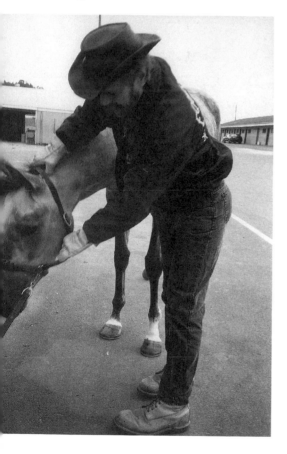

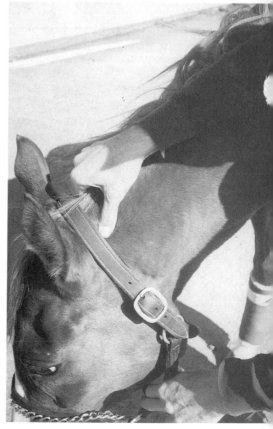

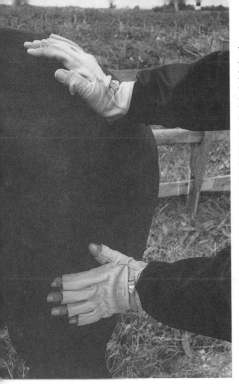

Working on the hind end. The left hand is the "protection-deflection" hand while the right hand is using palm pressure-release. If there is a height difference between you and the horse, use a hay bale for protection and height. In the second photograph, the right hand is squeezing and releasing, working down the hock, and the left hand is protecting-deflecting. The third photograph shows the right hand protecting-deflecting while the fingers of the left hand palpate the inner thigh and also does cross-fiber friction.

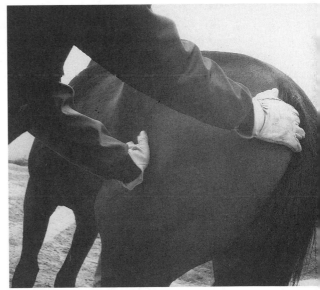

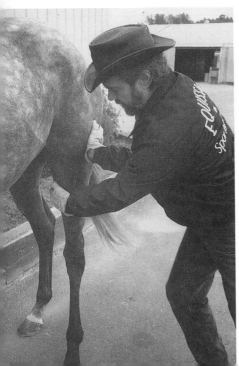

• EVALUATING YOUR HORSE •

While it would be convenient to have some kind of formula to be able to relate a specific type of injury to a specific type of usage, most times it is the unusual that perplexes trainers. Each trainer has his or her own tried-and-true methods for dealing with normal usage problems, whether it is the "hunter's bump," or the Thoroughbred's "left rear, right front." Dr. Meredith Snader has included acupressure meridian charts in Chapter One; if you're in doubt how to proceed, first try direct pressure along these lines.

Notice if the response in the horse is bilateral, in which case the problem might have a skeletal-alignment component. In that case, see Dr. Sharon Willoughby's chapter on chiropractic. If the response affects just one side or one limb, it could be the result of an accident. If it is on the diagonal, it is probably due to some motion that the animal is doing. You must take into account rider skills, tack, and any other variable that could be applicable.[5]

The first skill to develop is observation. Notice posture, gait, any obvious abnormalities, attitude, and "comfort factor." Does the animal rest one leg, or shift its weight frequently? Will it switch leads willingly? Is its disposition nervous, calm, or dull? Is it aggressive, or hiding in the back of the stall? Does it seem stiff? What is the stool like? Might the problem be a vitamin (digestive) deficiency, or something internal?

Secondly, you must ask questions. Are there any contributing factors? Has there been a slip, a fall, or a fight with another animal? What has been changed or done differently lately? Don't be surprised if it takes time to figure out the "why."[6] I have, on occasion, found suspected hoof problems to be coming from the shoulder. Evaluation is a process of elimination. By thoroughly feeling the muscle textures, it is easier to determine what is *not* the problem and to go on from there![7]

One easily overlooked cause of muscular problems is

Lifting the head to check for deflection. Repeat at least three times. If the head goes off to one side, that is the side with the tight muscle(s).

Mobilization of the head and neck. *Below Left:* The horse should not resist, but allow the weight of his head to rest in your hand or on your shoulder. Sometimes tickling his nose will relax him and facilitate turning. *Below Right.* Here the weight of his head is on my shoulder and in my hands and he is relaxed. Make sure the range is equal bilaterally.

shoes. Make sure that the feet are balanced, or all of the work you do on the muscles will quickly be undone! See that the hoof angles are the same all around. (How well would a woman walk in one high heel and one sneaker?) Did the problem develop shortly after shoeing? A stone bruise in the hoof can also cause behavior that seems like a muscular problem. Finally, different kinds of shoes can of themselves cause problems. Toe-grabs, for instance, can cause muscle strain. My advice is not to shoe a horse immediately before competition if it can be helped, because the animal needs time to adjust to new shoes.

I am also assuming that a veterinarian has examined the horse to determine that there is no chemical, structural, or biological basis for the animal's problems. If the problem appears to be muscular, the traditional medical approach calls for anti-inflammatories, muscle relaxants, painkillers, surgery, and/or rest depending on how severe and how chronic the problem is. Much better results can often be otained by going directly to the tight muscle and relaxing it. However, if the animal won't let you touch a particular area, or if he is apprehensive about your being there, a small amount of painkiller, as well as a large amount of patience, may be necessary.

My earlier background in massage, before I began working with horses, was fifteen years of working with humans, so I often make direct comparisons between horses and the human condition. Take, for example, the head-shy horse. Accepted wisdom, taught by stories like *Black Beauty*, has it that somewhere in the horse's life it was abused by a cruel handler. Yet I have seen head-shy horses that were foaled and raised by kind trainers. I worked on one horse that had come out of a race head-shy! A tape of the race showed why: In the final turn another horse had drifted out and slammed into him at full gallop, causing his head to fly upward and over his right shoulder in what we would call a classic case of whiplash. Many horses with bad attitudes could be suffering from the horse equivalent of a migraine headache. It is impossible to tell, but I have seen dramatic improvements in attitude following neck massage, enough to suggest that headache relief may have been the answer.[8] A predisposition to "tie-up" can also be relieved gradually by massage, and colic is also ameliorable.

• GO TO WORK •

Start with the neck of the animal and begin by gently stroking the area while speaking reassuringly. Follow the direction of the hair. Spend the first few minutes getting acquainted with the animal. Stroke (pet) slowly over larger and diverse areas and see if there is any guarding, apprehension, flinching, or muscle-twitching. You want to be working on about a three-foot "block" at a time, but do not maintain strict boundaries, since muscle problems usually include several groups and overlap into other areas before they become really noticeable. See what areas the horse eagerly presents to you and where he pulls away. Gently and gradually increase the intensity of the massage until a response is observed; record approximately how much pressure you are using and slowly decrease the intensity. Keep this baseline pressure and patiently work your way all around one side. Use compression and jostling. I sometimes pretend that I'm painting every inch of the horse. In fact, it may be a good idea to get out your favorite liniment and thoroughly rub it in. Vary your strokes and pressures while establishing a rhythm. You want to create a pattern of movements that the animal can anticipate and adapt to as it learns to trust you.

So, having started on the neck, you've loosened up the shoulders, withers, and rump, as well as the breast, legs, back, and all points in between. Now you are ready to continue around to the other side, moving your three-foot

Indicates nose to chest-shoulder junction. Movement should be free and accomplished in one continuous "swoop." Jostling will help loosen the neck if restriction is found, as will massaging the muscles on the opposite side.

work area about a foot at a time, so that there is always an overlap.

After the animal has been thoroughly loosened, manipulate the head several times, moving from up and back to down and in. See if there is a tendency to deflect to the left or right. Support the head by reaching over the nose and holding the halter and slowly assist the horse as you move the head from center to side. He should be able to touch his nose to the area of the anterior superficial pectoral muscle (chest-shoulder junction) and between the lateral head of the triceps and the latissimus dorsi (armpit). Don't force any movement, just note how easy the movement is.

Pick up a foreleg to see if there are any obvious restrictions to free motion. The forelegs should be able to stretch rearward to about 70 degrees, with the knee both bent and

Foreleg stretches. The pupose is to check for freedom of movement in the shoulder, knee, and ankle. The leg should move freely both fore and aft, as well as side to side. First, stretch the leg to the rear until the horse almost tries to step down on it. Then compress it upward and rotate the shoulder. Move the knee in a circle. Finally, pull the leg forward and upward until you feel the shoulder stretch out and he begins to allow you to hold some of his weight.

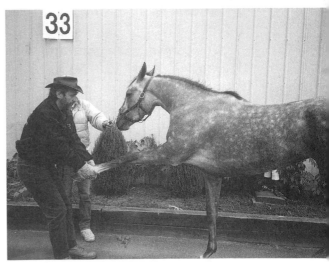

33

straight, without much discomfort. Stand in front, to one side, and lift the leg forward. Is it heavy or light? While lifting the forearm (ulna) parallel to the ground, grasp the splint bone behind the knee and push and pull. The shoulder should slide freely from front to back in a fluid movement. While in this position, gently swing the knee from side to side to see how tight the chest muscles are. Slowly extend the leg straight forward and pull away slowly and firmly. The horse should be able to tolerate this movement; he will probably pull back a little (as in tug of war) before finally releasing the shoulder completely and extending forward. If the horse begins to rear or back up, lower the hoof and try again at a shallower angle. Remember, you are looking for the side (muscles) that won't let go.

Establishing the range of motion of the hind end is a much more imposing task, but it too must be undertaken. Stand just behind the shoulder and indicate that you want to pick up the hind leg. Reach down behind the fetlock, lift the hoof and stretch it forward with the toe extended. It is a good sign if the horse attempts to extend the leg toward the foreleg and begins to place weight on it. Shift your grip to the area of the coronet in front and slowly walk the leg rearward. Keep a firm grip so that the horse can use you to maintain balance as it extends. It is well if you get a slight tug in response, but if the leg jerks away, the stifle/gaskin may have knurdles.

Finally, lift the tail and feel how flexible it is. (Be careful, especially with mares in season!) Move the tail from side to side and over the croup. It should be loose and able to curl upward like a dog's. If not, it means that there may be a problem in the buttocks.

Return to the head, reach slowly to the poll, and, with opposing thumb and fingers about 3 inches apart, alternately squeeze, press, and release on either side of the vertebrae. Continue at approximately half-inch intervals and move down the spine to the tail. You will probably get a flinching or twinging from several areas. See how

Hind leg stretches. Slowly pull the hind leg forward until the horse just begins to shift weight on it. Slowly move the leg from side to side while speaking words of encouragement. Stop just when the hoof barely touches the ground. Then if he is cooperative, without letting go, hold on to the leg and walk toward the rear, keeping the hoof low to the ground. When you get behind him, keep a firm pressure and pull the leg toward you and slightly upward. Watch his rump, and you will see the change in the muscles as he relaxes and extends. When you get full extension, praise him, and gradually release.

Checking the tail. The tail should be free and loose in all directions. You should be able to rotate it 360 degrees. The tail is a continuation of the spinal column, so restricted motion or a pain response can indicate problems in the lumbosacral area. Remember, the side being *extended* will produce the pain response.

they correlate with the areas that you got responses from previously. Make more mental notes.

On the next pass, you find and concentrate on the knurdles. All of the observations you have made up to this point can be incorporated into an overall perspective. Where was the animal most reactive? What movements were resisted? Since muscles pull in a straight line, along their length, it is a simple matter to begin a motion and to feel where tightening occurs.[9] Now feel along the length of the muscle and see how quickly you can find and identify the knurdle. Apply direct pressure, mixed with light percussion, on the exact center of the knurdle, and follow this with compression. Continue around the animal, addressing all of the areas where you noticed deficiencies. Remember the

Palpating the spine. Begin at the poll and squeeze and press. Release. Repeat the process at about one-inch intervals along the spine. Feel for lumps, swelling, or sensitivity. Work your way down the spine to the tail. Watch for twitching in the skin surface and always use your free hand to guard against kicks. Even the most gentle horse will react if you poke a "hot spot."

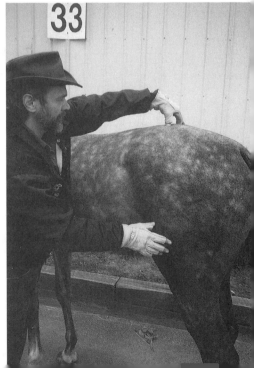

Don't forget the underbelly. Usually this is the area least affected by muscle strains, although it can be injured if the horse is spread-eagled on some slippery surface. Be careful, gentle (especially with a filly), and slowly rub in a circular motion to check for sensitivity. Do *not* use percussion or heavy pressure! An injury to this area requires light pressure and patience to gradually massage out.

house-restoration analogy? Now you are carefully filling and smoothing very deep but narrow cracks in imaginary plaster. It takes strength and patience to hold the pressure without repeatedly slipping off the right spot, but you will be rewarded when you finally feel the muscle begin to soften beneath your touch. Do not be surprised if this is accompanied by a deep sigh from the horse! As each area begins to soften, move on to the next. Be thorough. After all, this is the reason that you are here. This is why you made friends with the horse, why you are developing a working relationship, why you began in the first place!

When you are satisfied that you have left no hair un-turned, finish with long strokes, general compression, percussion, and kind words for the horse. Repeat the stretches and notice improvements in the range of motion. Finally, walk the horse for several minutes, or have it exercised lightly to accommodate the changes that you have facilitated.

Congratulations! You have just completed the hardest massage that you'll ever have to do: the first one. Perhaps some of the things you did made no sense, perhaps you were timid in your delivery. No matter! Now you have a general feel for what you are doing and a basis for comparison that can be applied to all future horses. As you build upon this and add other horses to your roster, seemingly random events will form patterns, and you can extract your own generalities and lessons. Remember, massage is just a series of approximations. Don't get discouraged if you don't work miracles the first (or second) time. Persevere and you will be rewarded.

· NOTES ·

1. To avoid any possible conflicts with the medical profession, I have coined the word "knurdle." Only a medical doctor or a veterinarian may diagnose, so I, as a layperson, look to find knurdles.

2. Meagher, Jack, *Beating Muscle Injuries for Horses.* Hamilton, Mass.: Hamilton Horse Associates, 1985.

3. I suggest that you buy some lightweight gloves and cut off the fingertips at midlength. Wearing these gloves will protect your knuckles and palms from abrasions until your skin toughens up a bit, while leaving your fingertips unrestricted and exposed.

4. The jury is still out on this one. One school of thought believes in short bursts of pressure (seven seconds), others believe in sustained pressure. I lean toward thirty seconds minimum.

5. Let me illustrate: I was asked to evaluate an imported show horse in Vermont that was hesitant to use his right foreleg properly. After examining the animal, I found he was sensitive in an area near the withers. I was puzzled: I had never known another horse to be sensitive there, and I could not account for it by his training or usage. Finally I asked about the saddle and pad. The rider was using a thin, high-tech foam pad with a very expensive saddle. I observed several half-moon indentations on the saddle pad corresponding to the same area as the horse's sensitivity. So I asked to see the saddle. The rider said there was no way that it could be the saddle because it was custom-made for the horse. When I examined it, I found that some screws had worked loose on the underside and were poking the horse in the shoulder, precisely where he was sore. Mas-

sage helped the soreness, and saddle repair "fixed" the problem.

6. I evaluated a horse for a weight-bearing hesitancy and could find nothing out of the ordinary to explain it. The muscles generally, and the shoulder in particular, seemed fine. Some time later I spoke to the trainer and learned the probable cause: an abscess that appeared and broke right under the frog just after the massage.

7. When I first began working with horses, I asked a well-known trainer for a few words of wisdom that would prove useful if I continued working with horses. He said, "Son, a horse will make a liar out of you every time." Keep an open mind!

8. Cribbing is another condition that I believe indicates neck problems. Although conventional wisdom says that it is a learned bad habit, several horses I have worked on stopped cribbing temporarily, or drastically reduced the habit, after massage!

9. Usually the other side; that is, if the head resists moving to the left, it means that the muscles on the right are holding it back.

HERBAL

IHOR JOHN BASKO, D.V.M.

Medical treatment is older than intelligence in man. The dog hunts the fields for his special grass medicine; the bear dresses the wound of her bear cub or fellow bear with as much intelligence as primitive man observes in his empirical practice. Primitive man does not know why his medicine cures; he simply knows that it does cure.

—M. C. Stevenson,
Ethnobotany of the Zuni Indians

INTRODUCTION

The horse is an herbivore that has evolved over millions of years from a browsing forest animal to a grazing animal with the freedom to roam the grasslands and prairies. As the glaciers receded during the last Ice Age, more and more grasslands were available to all grazing animals (bison, antelope, gazelles, cattle, sheep, goats, and horses), and they proliferated throughout the steppes of Eurasia and Mongolia, the African savannahs, and the prairies of North America. Depending upon soil and climate conditions, different kinds of grasses (wheat, rye, fescue, barley, rice) and plants were available to eat. Instinct led the horses to eat plants that helped them survive. They moved from one area to another searching for beneficial plants and grasses.

Early man came out of the forests and began to hunt creatures that roamed the plains. Horses were hunted as food. Man's relationship with the horse changed when he discovered that the animal could be ridden to hunt other animals, like bison, at greater distances. The horse became extremely valuable. Man and beast lived closer together. The domestication of the horse some 10,000 years or more ago led primitive humans to the responsibilities of feeding, caring for, and and healing these animals, using the very same plant medicines on the horse as they used on themselves.

Many medicinal plants grew on the prairies and grasslands. These plants might have included gentian, red clover, dandelion, poppies, plantain, milkweed, thistle, and wild onion. In those times, human beings lived close to nature. Their survival demanded that they be aware of it and be able to adapt to changes in nature. Out of necessity, they learned the different properties of plants.

Early herbal medicine developed by the trial-and-error method. Medicine men and women tested plants on themselves and their animals. Some took herbs and became stronger and were revered as shamans for their magical healing abilities. Others died in the testing of new plants, but the information was passed on to other family members. The secrets of the healing qualities of plants were kept within the families.

In China and India families of healers kept records, developed techniques of processing herbs that made them more potent and which could be stored for long periods of time without spoiling.

Over many centuries, the Chinese developed the most sophisticated and systematic approach to the use of medicinal herbs known today. The Emperor Shen Nung (c. 3,500 B.C.) and his administration tested many many kinds of herbs to ascertain their healing properties.

The Greeks, under Alexander the Great (356–323 B.C.), brought back from China and Egypt many herbal remedies and treatments to the Mediterranean states. After the Ro-

mans conquered the Greeks, they spread this information throughout Europe and the British Isles.

During the Dark Ages and the Renaissance, the monks of the Church kept records and used herbs for healing and for making salves and medicinal spirits. The knowledge remained static and declined, however, until the discovery of the Americas.

From the Indians of Central and South America, the Europeans learned about anesthetic plants and how to treat malaria. Indians of North America taught the settlers how to use plants for problems of childbirth and in the treatment of infections and pneumonia. Also, new methods of using and making salves, liniments, and poultices were introduced by the Native Americans, who better understood the healing powers of plants, because they lived so closely with them.

Until the beginning of the twentieth century, physicians, veterinarians, and other healers were dependent upon herbs for the well-being and treatment of their patients. What has happened to the credibility of herbal medicine since then? The Industrial Revolution in Europe during the eighteenth and nineteenth centuries took human beings away from the countrysides and farms and brought them into the cities to work and live away from nature. Human beings sought to "harness" nature's powers in order to make *machines* work. As the lifestyles of people changed, science and medicine became more technical and less natural.

The early part of the twentieth century gave rise to the "Chemical Revolution," and some of the first drugs and antibiotics were discovered inadvertently by chemical and textile companies in Europe. During the First and Second World Wars these same companies helped produce chemicals not only as deadly weapons but also as medicines to heal wounds and infections on the battlefield. The production of healing drugs became a business, and compa-

nies sought cheaper ways to make synthetic drugs from active ingredients in plants.

Although much good has come from the use of synthetic drugs in medicine, they have acquired an incredibly large influence in our culture. Indeed, we live in a drug-dependent society. We take over-the-counter drugs as readily as we brush our teeth. We have forgotten our "roots"! Our culture has removed itself from nature and the gifts it brings, so much so that we don't trust anything that isn't packaged in a plastic bottle with a tamper-proof seal on it! Many of the drug companies support the medical and veterinary universities while at the same time pushing their products on the staffs and students. Much disinformation about the credibility of herbal medicine, acupuncture, chiropractic, and nutrition has been spread by companies and medical organizations that feel financially threatened. Consequently, only a few pockets of herbal medical knowledge survive today in the United States. Only the Native Americans, the hill people of the Eastern states, and immigrant farmers and forest dwellers who grew up living close to the earth still use herbal remedies in their lives.

• REDISCOVER HERBS •

After President Richard Nixon's visit to China in 1973, the doors to new possibilities for healing were opened, especially the ancient art of acupuncture as practiced by the Chinese. I was lucky to participate in a research study of veterinary acupuncture through the University of California in Los Angeles in 1975. Fifty other veterinarians from eight different states also participated. This project changed my way of thinking about medicine. Acupuncture offered a revolutionary way to cure paralysis and alleviate pain without drugs or surgery. With this knowledge I

would be better able to serve my animal patients and give their owners alternatives besides surgery or euthanasia.

My teacher at the time, Dr. Sang Shin, whose father was a veterinarian in Korea, told me that Chinese herbal medicines were even more powerful healers than acupuncture. It stimulated me to seek out people who knew about herbs.

I began my study and research of Western herbs in San Jose in 1976 with the aid of my mentor and friend, Dr. Sid Golinsky, who had taught pharmacy and pharmacognosy at the University of California, Berkeley. Dr. Golinsky inspired me to learn about herbs and to use them on animals, mainly horses at that time. I discovered how well horses respond to the treatments. The herbs seemed to enhance my acupuncture treatments for pain and stiffness and gave the animals more energy, shinier coats, and happier dispositions. I decided to devote my life to the study, the use, and the growing of herbal plants.

• WHAT ARE HERBS? •

To quote another mentor of mine who introduced me to Chinese herbal medicine, Dr. Stephen Chang: "Herbs are plants, animals, and minerals that are ingested or applied externally to the human body to prevent and heal physical illnesses by adjusting the flow of vital energy and supplying the basic materials for regeneration of body cells or tissues."

Enzymes and trace minerals that act as catalysts in the body, stimulating the regeneration of cells, are some of the most important elements contributed by medicinal plants. The modern-day horse typically lives in a restricted environment, dependent upon the human beings for its sustenance. Most suburban horses do not have access to grazing on pastures; they are fed processed grasses and grains in the form of cubes and pellets. The nutritiousness of these feeds depends upon the quality of the soil in which the raw materials were grown, on the season of the year in which they were harvested, and on the handling and storage of the feeds. The mineral composition and organic content of soil varies from place to place, depending on such factors as drought, erosion, overirrigation, salinization, and chemical residues. All this affects the fertility of the soil and the quality of the feedstuffs and pasture grown on it. Quality of feed is especially critical to growing foals, yearlings, and lactating mares. Horses, like all herbivores, need to eat "live" food. Horses given the freedom to roam supplement themselves with a variety of minerals from the soil and plants in different locations.

It is my belief that certain kinds of colic, asthma, many forms of arthritis, and a shortened life span are in part the result of keeping horses in small stalls and paddocks where they cannot graze. However, with the human population explosion, the shortage of land, and dwindling supplies of food worldwide, we cannot afford the luxury of having rich pastures for all our horses.

The alternative is to supplement the diet of horses with herbal plants that possess regenerative properties and catalytic actions. Many of these can be grown in your own backyard or stable areas. Others can be ordered by mail or obtained from health food stores or stores serving a Chinese clientele.

Herbs can be given to horses mixed in their feed fresh, or in the form of powders, or as a brewed tea. Feeding the horse will take a little more time, but the benefits outweigh the small inconvenience.

• AGED HORSES •

When I first started practicing acupuncture and herbal medicine, the people who called me were those with aged horses. These horses were stiff, arthritic, unthrifty looking, but they had gentle disposition and were much loved by their owners. What can be done for such animals? Some people, believing there are no alternatives, would choose to euthanize. There *are* alternatives to try, however, one of which is the use of herbal supplements.

Older horses get stiff and arthritic because cellular and metabolic waste products accumulate and solidify in and around the joints, causing inflammation to the cartilage, ligaments, and surrounding soft tissue. This degenerative process is further aggravated by previous injuries, scar tissue, and poor circulation due to inactivity. Many people will retire these horses from exercise, but exercise is what they need to maintain good circulation and a positive mental attitude.

The first older horse I treated, named Polly, had spent her life working with children as a vaulting pony. As Polly aged, she got progressively stiffer because of ringbone and a sore back. Finally, the owner had to retire her. This retirement broke Polly's heart. She missed the contact with the children and wanted to be ridden by them and her owner. After a series of acupuncture treatments for pain, Polly was maintained on herbal teas and powders, specifically the two infusions whose recipes appear in the box on page 185: Spring Cleaning Tea, and Arthritis Formula. This older horse became a happier horse who was able to be ridden by children and her owner again on a part-time basis, adding several more enjoyable years to her life.

Herbs are given to horses to improve circulation and to nourish and improve the functions of the kidneys, liver, intestines, and blood. The formulas that helped Polly contain tonic herbs that promote the functioning of the internal organs (dandelion, sassafras, red clover, parsley, and juniper). Wild yam root and yucca provide nutrients that the horse uses to make anti-inflammatory steroid hormones for the control of pain.

Other herbs cleanse the blood and digestive organs (buchu leaves, slippery elm, sarsaparilla). After three to six weeks on the Spring Cleaning Tea, the coat should become shinier, and the animal's attitude brighter. If the horse is still lame and stiff, start him on the Arthritis Formula for another three to six weeks. When improvement occurs, gradually decrease the dosage to one-half of the original dose, and maintain the horse at that level. If the animal has a chance of improving, it will occur within the first three months.

Horses love taking the tea mixed with their regular grain, sweet feed, or bran. The herb powder contains many trace minerals that are missing in the horse's regular feed and satisfies the horse's craving for them. If they were free to roam, most horses would find the plants they need to satisfy their mineral needs.

The Spring Cleaning Tea is good for horses of all ages as a way to cleanse the body of waste products. Horses that have been inactive in the wintertime and those that have been subjected to many different drug and pesticide treatments can benefit greatly from a three-week program. As a preventative program, a twice-a-year treatment can be very beneficial to maintain the integrity of the internal organs.

Another herb that can be used in a preventative program for horses young and old is American Ginseng (*Panax quinquefolius*). This herb was sought after extensively in the woodlands of Eastern Canada, Wisconsin, West Virginia, Tennessee, Kentucky, and Georgia during the 1700s as a source of income. People scoured the countryside looking for this herb to sell to merchants who would then sell it to the Chinese. Daniel Boone was one of the men who hunted this valuable plant and made a small fortune sell-

Spring Cleaning Tea

Dandelion (*Taraxacum officinale*)	root powder	2 cups
Parsley (*Petroselinum* spp.)	root powder	1 cup
Juniper (*Juniperis communis*)	berries	1 cup
Sassafras (*Sassafras albidum*)	root bark	1 cup
Buchu (*Barosma betulina*)	leaves	2 cups
Bearberry (*Arctostaphylos uva-ursi*)	leaves	1 cup
Slippery elm (*Ulmus fulva*)	bark	2 cups
Red clover (*Trifolium pratense*)	flowers	4 cups

Mix all the above herbs together well and store in a covered plastic container. To prepare the tea, add 2 cups of boiling water to 6 tablespoons of the mixed powder and let steep for 20 minutes, then mix with feed.

Arthritis Formula

Yucca (*Yucca* spp.)	root powder	2 cups
Wild yam (*Dioscorea villosa*)	root powder	2 cups
Chaparral (*Larrea divaricata*)	leaves	1 cup
Comfrey (*Symphytum officinale*)	root	2 cups
Sarsaparilla (*Smilax officinalis*)	root	1 cup
Horsetail (*Equisetum* spp.)	plant powder	½ cup

Add 2 cups of boiling water to 4 tablespoons of the mixed herbs and let steep for 20 minutes. Mix with feed twice daily.

ing it. This herb is beneficial for tonifying the digestive system, lungs, and kidneys.

American Ginseng root can be purchased in Chinese herbal stores very easily. A root four to six years old, a half-inch thick and 6 inches long, is boiled in one gallon of water for one hour. When the tea is cool, it is decanted into a glass bottle. More water is added (a half-gallon) to the remaining root and simmered for another hour; when cool, that tea is decanted and mixed with the first batch. Give the horse one cup daily for as long as the tea lasts (seven or eight days). Repeat this tonifying treatment every three to four months.

Another beneficial herb to brew along with the American ginseng is Chinese licorice root (*Glycyrrhiza uralensis*). This inexpensive tonic herb is beneficial for all the internal organs and is noted for its detoxifying effects. A half-cup of the dried roots of this plant, simmered together with one American ginseng root, can be one of the best preventative treatments for colic, lung infections, asthma, and muscle tension.

I have emphasized the use of American and European herb plants, because these medicinal plants are the easiest to obtain and grow. (Please see the lists of reference books and herb suppliers at the end of this chapter). In my own practice, when prescribing formulas for sick horses, I make up formulas containing Chinese medicinal herbs. These herbs have the strongest effects and their use requires extensive study and experience.

▪ WOUND CARE ▪

What do horse owners associate with fences, nails, barbed wire, sheet metal, and rocks?

The answer: "Cuts! Scrapes! Gouges! . . . and Wounds!!" If you own horses, the chances are great that sometime, in some place, a wound will be staring you in the face! Many times injuries happen on weekends, late at night, or far away on a distant trail. It may take your veterinarian many hours to get to your horse. What you do in the first twelve hours will determine the course of events.

The skin is torn and broken, the soft underlying tissues are bruised, swollen, and oozing blood, and the horse is standing through the fence with a wild look in his eyes . . . What are you going to do? First take a few deep breaths and calm yourself down, because this is very beneficial in calming down your horse and preventing further injury. After rescuing your horse from the fence and getting him relaxed, take him to a quiet, comfortable place and get some help.

For effective results, it is important to understand the basic steps of wound healing. Four phases of wound treatment are:

1. CLEAN
2. DISINFECT
3. HEAL
4. PROTECT

How you clean a wound is very important. All dirt and debris must be removed without being forced deeper into the wound. This can be done with the aid of gauze sponges, tweezers (boiled), Q-Tips, or a spray bottle. The wound can be cleaned with drinking water, clean ocean water, or a diluted mixture (1:1) of three percent hydrogen peroxide solution and aloe vera juice. A mild tea made from goldenseal root (*Hydrastis canadensis*) or plantain leaves (*Plantago* spp.), administered through a spray bottle, is an effective way of cleaning and disinfecting at the same time. The pressure from the "squirt" removes dirt efficiently. To make the teas, simply add one teaspoon of goldenseal powder or one tablespoon of dried plantain leaves (two tablespoons if fresh) to a cup of boiling water and let it steep for twenty minutes.

After cleaning comes disinfecting. Any contaminating harmful organisms that may have entered the wound with the dirt and debris must be killed. This can be accomplished the standard way by using either Betadine or Novasan disinfecting veterinary solutions. If these solutions are not available, making a tea from goldenseal or plantain, using Australian Tea Tree Oil (*Melaleuca alternifolia*), or applying unfiltered, uncooked honey can work very well. If the wound is deeper than 1 inch, avoid getting the chemical disinfectants down that deep. They will create irritation and delay wound healing. Of course, these herbal remedies will not combat tetanus spores, so your horse may need a tetanus booster and some penicillin from the veterinarian.

The third phase of treating a wound is healing. This is the most important of all the steps, and the outcome is influenced to a great extent by the cleaning and disinfecting of the wound. To facilitate healing, a "healing environment" must be created. This involves keeping the wound moist and clean, which provides an organic medium for cell regeneration and prevents infections from harmful bacteria. The best way to create a healing environment is with special herbal fresh plants. Antibiotic ointments, the choice of many, only satisfy the criteria of preventing infections and keeping the wound clean. Because of their chemical nature, the ointments slow down the healing process, however.

Research on a Hawaiian medicinal plant, noni or Indian mulberry (*Morinda citrifolia*), at the University of Hawaii has uncovered an enzyme that facilitates regeneration of damaged cells. This enzyme accomplishes cell regeneration by supplying a necessary nutrient to the damaged cells. Comfrey, plantain, noni leaves, and aloe vera pulp contain many enzymes for healing. These plants, used FRESH, singly or in combination, as a poultice, offer one of the best treatments for wound healing. Plantain has the added advantage of helping to stop minor bleeding and the oozing of blood.

To make a poultice, take one cup of fresh clean leaves of comfrey, a half-cup of plantain leaves, and a half-cup of boiling water and reduce them to a paste with a mortar and pestle or in a blender. Apply this paste directly on the wound and around the wound. If the wound is deeper than

1 inch, make a herbal tea from these plants and flush it into the wound. If these plants are not available, soak some clean roll gauze (3 to 4 inches wide) in aloe vera juice (obtainable at most health food stores) and wrap it around the wound. If an aloe vera plant is available, scrape the pulp from the inside of the leaf into the wound and wrap it with gauze.

Another Chinese remedy to have in your first-aid kit is Yunnan Paiyao powder (also available in herb shops in Chinese neighborhoods). This powder has wonderful properties for controlling hemorrhage and preventing infections without delaying healing. Simply put a half-teaspoon or more into a wound and bandage.

Protection of the wound from further injury and infection is the final phase of wound treatment. Bandaging a wound is both simple and important. After the herb dressing is applied to the wound, cover the wound with either square gauze sponges (4″ x 4″), or a nonstick adherent dressing (Telfa pad). Next (third layer), secure the dressing with either cotton roll gauze (3″–4″ wide), a clean strip of cotton, or a bandanna.

The final layer on the bandage is the tape. If possible, do not apply tape directly over the wound, because air needs to get to the wound. Use 2-inch-wide elastic-type bandage tape to keep the gauze or bandanna from falling off. If the wound must be taped over to keep the bandage in place, use porous tape only.

If the wound seeps much fluid, you will have to change the bandage twice a day, and apply fresh poultice and clean new gauze after rinsing out the wound with tea.

The above treatments will help facilitate healing and help your horse until the veterinarian comes. Generally, it is best to suture the wound in the first twelve hours after injury. After this time the wound starts organizing into scar tissue and it becomes harder to suture. This treatment will give you and your veterinarian a little more time. Improperly treated wounds most commonly result in the production of excessive granulation tissue, better known as proud flesh. When this occurs, supervision and treatment by a veterinarian are essential to successful healing. Deep punctures and wounds usually require treatment with antibiotics and tetanus toxoid or antitoxin injections by your veterinarian.

▪ BRUISES, MUSCLE AND ▪ TENDON STRAINS

Probably some of the most misunderstood methods of treating horses are the uses of liniments and poultices. When an injury such as a tendon strain, muscle tear, or bruise from a kick occurs, most people would agree that treatment with ice and running cold water is the appropriate first-aid to administer during the first day or two. What to do after this is a matter of disagreement among veterinarians and experienced horse people.

What happens when the underlying structures of the skin are "insulted" by an injury? Muscles, tendons, fasciae, blood vessels, and soft tissues have been macerated, torn, and stretched apart by a force greater than the tissues could bear. Blood starts to leak out of capillaries, veins, and arteries. Damaged cells also lose their cellular fluid and everything drains into the injured area. The pain the horse experiences is due to torn nerve sections in the tissue of the muscles and tendons, and to pressure on these nerves from the fluid that has built up in the area. Because the circulation has been impaired, the tissues continue to swell from blood and cellular fluid, causing more pain and a delayed healing response. It will take a few days for the horse to begin to reestablish a little circulation from the ailing capillaries.

Treatment with ice and cold running water helps to

constrict the damaged tissues and broken blood vessels, thus decreasing the amount of seepage that is present. This treatment cools the leg and reduces the inflammation caused by the pressure of the swelling. To help remove stagnant blood, clots, and cellular fluid so that healing can be accelerated, cooling poultices and compresses should be used to draw out the fluids. The poultices and compresses change the osmotic pressure at the site of the injury.

Poultices should be made from fresh plants. The most healing poultices use comfrey (leaves), aloe vera (gel), plantain (leaves), and noni (leaves and fruit). These fresh plants can be used singly or in combination. The leaves have to be macerated in a blender or with a mortar and pestle. Add a little boiling water to make the mixture pasty; add some powder of slippery elm bark or comfrey root to the mixture to make it thicker. Apply this poultice right after the cold-water treatment and secure it in place on the site of the injury with roll gauze. This must be changed twice a day. A pressure bandage using an Ace-type wrap over the gauze and poultice may be necessary when a large area of swelling is present below the knee or hock. Care must be taken not to put the wrap on too tight, thus restricting the blood supply to the area.

A Chinese remedy I keep on hand when I don't have the time to make a fresh herb poultice is Wan Hua Oil. A little bottle of this medicine is easily acquired in Chinese-style herb shops. After running cold water or ice on the area, the leg should be dried with a towel and then this oil massaged into the injured and swollen area using circular, light, gentle strokes. After five to ten minutes of massaging, a dressing of roll gauze and an Ace-type bandage should cover the leg overnight.

Gentle massage promotes healing by stimulating the movement of stagnant fluids out of the injury site through improved circulation. The medicinal properties of the herbal oil (vulnerary) encourages the repair of broken cells and capillaries. At this stage of treatment, I would also prescribe a Chinese herbal tea for the animal to drink that would aid circulation, reduce pain, and stimulate healing. This tea would be individually formulated by one specific for each animal and would include Tang Kuei Root, Pseudoginseng Root and a variety of other Chinese herbs.

After the swelling starts to reduce, continue using this oil massaged into the injury site two or three times daily without wrapping the leg for several days.

After a week or two, all of the swelling and pain should be reduced. The injured tissues are continuing to heal, with some "leftovers" of dead tissue and blood clots that are organizing into scar tissue. This scar tissue delays healing and will continue to cause pain in the area even after the damaged tissues have healed. The horse may seem fine at the walk and short trot, but with any more exertion, he experiences pain, inflammation, and tenderness to touch.

Now is the time to consider the use of poultices or liniments that warm and stimulate the injury by increasing circulation.

Numotizine and Antiphlogistine are some commercial poultice preparations that can be used at this time. A poultice made from fresh mashed ginger root can be applied directly and secured with roll gauze overnight. These should be changed daily and the leg washed before more poultice is applied. These treatments need to be continued for three to seven days.

An easier method of treatment is the use of Chinese herbal liniments that are massaged into the injured area two to three times a day. The leg must not be wrapped, as this may cause blistering of the skin. The products that I use most commonly are: Zheng Gu Shui, Wood Lock Medicated Balm, Po Som On Oil, and Tiger Balm. After application of the liniments, heat can be applied in the form of a hot, wet towel for ten to twenty minutes. This not only feels good but increases the flow of blood to the area. It is important to follow this treatment with light massage and gentle stretching for best results. I recommend this program before and after strenuous events that your horse is participating in.

Chronic problems lasting three months or more probably need special attention from a veterinarian who is skilled in the use of acupuncture and laser therapy. These problems are due mostly to the incomplete healing of tissues and the organization of scar tissue underlying the normal tissues. After acupuncture, recommended follow-up treatments are as follows:

1. application of alternating warm (five minutes) and cold (one minute) water on the injury site; repeated three times, twice a day;

2. followed by Chinese liniment massaged into the area for five to ten minutes;

3. then stretching the muscles and tendons gently for ten minutes near the site of the injury.

The ailing leg is wrapped with an Ace-type bandage to protect and support the healing tissues while the horse is exercised lightly for about twenty to thirty minutes every day.

After one to two weeks, progress should be seen or more extensive treatments from your veterinarian will be needed.

· FIRST-AID KIT ·

A first-aid kit is a must for all horse owners and should be kept at the pasture where your horse is located or in your car at all times. It should include the following items:

hydrogen peroxide
wound ointments
(Furacin, Aloe Heal)
poultices (Numotizine)
surgical scrub (Novasan)
Epsom salts
Chinese liniments
Rescue Remedy
homeopathic Ledum
Butazolidin or aspirin
Q-Tips
spray bottles
4″ x 4″ gauze pads
3″ or 4″ roll gauze
3″ or 4″ Ace bandage
duct tape
tourniquets
wire cutters

hot/cold packs
aloe vera juice
Betadine solution
rubbing alcohol
Wan Hua Oil
homeopathic Arnica
Yunnan Paiyao powder
homeopathic Hypericum
tweezers
cotton balls
goldenseal powder
nonstick Telfa pads
Vetrap
2″ porous tape
bandage scissors
cotton diapers
pliers
Swiss Army knife

• THE PREGNANT MARE •

Quite often I am called upon by worried clients to check a pregnant mare that was due to foal five days earlier. When a mare is late foaling, it is usually because of faulty record-keeping by the owners or because the mare is not "ready." A mare may not be ready due to the positioning of the fetus, emotional stress, or insufficient strength in the uterine muscles.

Unlike human medicine, where mothers often are induced into labor, this procedure is not normally performed on horses. Control of the hormonal system of horses by the use of synthetic drugs and hormones may be practical in large-scale breeding operations, but it does not serve the best interests of the animals.

Pregnant mares should be supplied with the necessary

trace minerals, good-quality feed, protein, and plants. Supplementing the pregnant mare with herbal mixes during the last three months of pregnancy promotes the health of both the mare and the fetus.

The herbal mix for mares consists of five ingredients, the first of which is fresh or dried comfrey leaves. This plant has deep roots that extract many minerals from the soil. The leaves mixed in daily rations will provide protein, calcium, phosphorus, iron, vitamin A, and manganese in healthy amounts to the mare.

The second ingredient, leaves of the red raspberry (*Rubus strigosus*), is known to prevent miscarriage and labor pains and helps to increase milk production. The leaves are also soothing to the digestive system. Both leaves and fruit contain a citrate of iron that helps to produce healthy blood and to control hemorrhaging at birth.

To the comfrey and red raspberry leaves add flowers of the red clover (*Trifolium pratense*) and chamomile (*Anthemis nobilis*). These stimulate circulation to the uterus, nerves, and stomach, promoting a good appetite and improving digestion.

The last ingredient in the formula is the sea vegetable, dulse (*Rhodymenia palmata*), which provides a rich assortment of vitamins and minerals and is more nutritious than many of the available horse products containing kelp.

The herbs are mixed in the following proportions:

        Comfrey leaves ....1 lb.
        Red raspberry leaves ....1 lb.
        Chamomile flowers ....½ lb.
        Red clover flowers ....½ lb.
        Dulse powder ....¼ lb.

These herbs are available through bulk herb distributors in dry form; they can be stored in a cool, dry place in plastic buckets that have tight-fitting lids.

The dosage to give your mare depends upon her condition. Generally, half to one cup a day of this mixture combined with sweet feed or bran is adequate for most horses. Commence supplementing the mare with the herbal mix around her seventh month of pregnancy and continue supplementing her for two months *after* foaling. Horses in poor condition, that have histories of prolonged labor, or are older than eighteen years can have up to four cups daily, which is gradually reduced as the horse's condition visually improves.

It is advantageous to grow your own comfrey, red clover, chamomile, and red raspberry. These can be dried or given fresh to eat. When feeding fresh herbs, double the amounts listed in the formula.

If you have a mare that is "trying" to get pregnant without success, try supplementing her with the herbal mix for six months, then attempt breeding again. If the mare does not take, then it "weren't to be" . . . as they say where I come from.

Blue cohosh (*Caulophyllum thalictroides*) was taken by Native American women in their last month of pregnancy. Mares that have had problems foaling or mares carrying their first foals may benefit from the use of this root, which helps to dilate the uterus. Mix one tablespoon of the powdered root in with the feed daily during the last week the mare is due to foal.

A veterinarian should check the pregnant mare during her last month, to ensure that everything is well within her.

The book list on page 199 will guide you in discovering more of the truths that herbs have to give us. I hope these books and your experience using and growing the plants will bring you "closer to the Earth."

• THE FUTURE •

Herbal medicine has recently made a comeback in global consciousness beyond that of a mere fad. One reason is that people are attracted more than ever to things of nature, because they are aware that we are fast losing the forests, the jungles, and the special places that we need in order to experience the beauty of our planet. Many of us "naturalists" worry that the solutions to numerous ailments will soon become extinct as these special places all over the world are burned and laid waste.

Conventional medical institutions are desperately investigating cures for cancer, AIDS, and heart disease. The tropical rain forests hold great potential for the discovery of new medicines from plants. The possibilities of finding those cures are diminishing as our ecosystems and natural plant environments diminish.

The contribution that plant medicine has made to mankind, currently and over the centuries, has been significant, and has passed the test of time. There is great promise for the use of medicinal plants in the future of veterinary medicine, and the increased interest in medicinal plants shown by veterinarians and physicians is encouraging. Refinements and more research are needed to continue this evolution in equine herbal medicine.

God and nature provide for all that ails us and our animals through the plant kingdom of Earth. We grow the food we eat, and we must discover and grow the medicines that heal us.

> *And to every beast of the earth,*
> *and to every fowl of the air,*
> *and to every thing that creepeth upon the earth*
> *wherein there is life,*
> *I have given every green herb for meat:*
> *and it was so . . .*
> *Genesis 1:30*

▪ BULK HERB SOURCES ▪

Indiana Botanic Gardens,
  Inc.
P.O. Box 5
Hammond, IN 46325

Meadowbrook Herb
  Garden
93 Kingstown Road
Wyoming, RI 02898

Revere Animal Supply
301 North Brandon,
  Unit 10
Fallbrook, CA 92028

Trinity Herb Company
P.O. Box 199
Bodega, CA 94922

Well Sweep Herb Farm
451 Mount Bethel Road
Port Murray, NJ 07865

World-Wide Herb Ltd.
11 Sainte Catherine Street
  East
Montreal 129 Canada

▪ BIBLIOGRAPHY ▪

Bavestrelli, Mirella. *Color Treasury of Herbs.* London: Crescent Books, 1972.

Castleman, M. "Ginseng Revered & Reviled." *The Herb Quarterly*, Winter issue, 1990.

Christopher, John R. *School of Natural Healing.* Provo, Utah: BiWorld Publishers, 1976.

Edward, Elwyn H. *Encyclopedia of the Horse.* London: Octopus Books, 1977.

Fox, Morgenthau H. *Gardening with Herbs for Flavor and Fragrance.* New York: Dover Publications, 1970.

Fulder, Stephen. *The Tao of Medicine.* New York: Destiny Books, 1980.

Gibbons, Euell. *Stalking the Good Life.* New York: David McKay Company, 1971.

Heath, M., R. F. Barnes, and D. S. Metcalfe. *Forages: The Science of Grassland Agriculture.* Ames, Iowa: Iowa State University Press, 1985.

Hylton, William H. *The Rodale Herb Book. How to Use, Grow, and Buy Nature's Miracle Plants.* Emmaus, Pa.: Rodale Press, 1974.

Kimmens, Andrew. *Tales of the Ginseng.* New York: William Morrow, 1975.

Krochmal, Arnold, and Connie Krochmal. *A Guide to the Medicinal Plants of the United States.* New York: Quadrangle, 1973.

Lewis, Lon P. *Feeding and Care of the Horse.* Philadelphia: Lea & Febiger, 1982.

Lust, John. *The Herb Book.* New York: Bantam Books, 1974.

Millspaugh, Charles F. *American Medicinal Plants.* New York: Dover Publications, 1974.

Mother Earth News Staff. *The Mother Earth News Almanac.* New York: Bantam Books, 1973.

Teeguarden, Ron. *Chinese Tonic Herbs.* Tokyo: Japan Publications, 1984.

Tierra, Michael. *Planetary Herbology.* Santa Fe: Lotus Press, 1988.

———. *The Way of Herbs.* Santa Cruz, Calif.: 1980.

Time-Life Books. *Grasslands and Tundra.* Alexandria, Va.: 1985.

Weatherford, Jack. *Indian Givers.* New York: Fawcett, 1988.

INDEX

Numbers in *italic* refer to illustrations.